Love and Loss

ALSO BY SCOTT H. LONGERT

No Money, No Beer, No Pennants: The Cleveland Indians and Baseball in the Great Depression

Bad Boys, Bad Times: The Cleveland Indians and Baseball in the Prewar Years, 1937–1941

Victory on Two Fronts: The Cleveland Indians and Baseball through the World War II Era

Cy Young: An American Baseball Hero

LOVE AND LOSS

The Short Life of Ray Chapman

Scott H. Longert

OHIO UNIVERSITY PRESS

ATHENS

Ohio University Press, Athens, Ohio 45701
ohioswallow.com
© 2024 by Ohio University Press
All rights reserved

To obtain permission to quote, reprint, or otherwise reproduce
or distribute material from Ohio University Press publications,
please contact our rights and permissions department at
(740) 593-1154 or (740) 593-4536 (fax).

Printed in the United States of America
Ohio University Press books are printed on acid-free paper ∞ ™

Library of Congress Cataloging-in-Publication Data
Names: Longert, Scott, author.
Title: Love and loss : the short life of Ray Chapman / Scott H.
   Longert.
Description: Athens, Ohio : Ohio University Press, [2024] | Includes
   bibliographical references and index.
Identifiers: LCCN 2024017245 | ISBN 9780821425688 (hardcover) |
   ISBN 9780821425664 (paperback) | ISBN 9780821425671 (pdf)
Subjects: LCSH: Chapman, Ray, 1891–1920. | Baseball players—United
   States—Biography. | Shortstop (Baseball)—United States. | Sports
   injuries—United States. | Cleveland Indians (Baseball team)—
   History—20th century. | Mays, Carl, 1891–1971. | United States—
   Baseball—History—20th century.
Classification: LCC GV865.C423 L66 2024 | DDC 796.357092 [B]—
   dc23/eng/20240427
LC record available at https://lccn.loc.gov/2024017245

Contents

Plates follow page 60

Acknowledgments

About twenty-seven years ago I began researching the life of Addie Joss, in hopes of authoring a story readers might enjoy and learn from. Through some luck it came to be, and my career was off and running. And it's still going three decades later.

Rather than concentrating on one individual, I managed to complete four additional works on Cleveland baseball history, with a break to write a Cy Young bio. With this telling of the Ray Chapman story, I have come to an understanding. I have returned to the place where I started. Both Addie and Ray were fine, upstanding men, great ballplayers who passed away much too soon. I believed in 1996 that Addie's story needed to be told, and two years ago I thought the same of Ray. Now, though, I believe it's a good time to put the pen down and reflect on a wonderful career I could never have imagined when I was a relatively young man.

My sincere thanks go to the staff at Ohio University Press for their continued support. Whether it be editorial, sales, or marketing, I could not have asked for a better group of people to assist me along the way. Their help with my four previous books will always be much appreciated.

My gratitude to the libraries in Davenport, Iowa; Herrin, Illinois; Toledo, Ohio; and Owensboro, Kentucky, for their willingness to help me with fresh material on Ray's early life. Special thanks to the librarians at Cleveland Public Library for their research help during the pandemic. The library was closed to the public at the time, but the staff looked up the newspaper dates I requested and emailed the information to me. Without them I would still be writing.

I am thankful to be friends with Jeremy Feador, the Cleveland Guardians team historian. Throughout my research time Jeremy shared information with me and suggested areas for me to pursue. He is a first-rate historian whom the Guardians are fortunate to have.

Many thanks to Bruce Milla for providing me with original photos of Ray's teammates. Bruce has been my go-to guy for Cleveland baseball photos over the last few years. His collection of baseball images is fantastic.

To my extended family, Gordon and Christopher, along with my new great-niece and great-nephew, Carolyn and Cameron: may you all grow up to be wonderful, caring people like your parents. I have no doubt whatsoever you will. I now have enough great-nieces and nephews for a basketball team with two bench players. Though we are just shy of a complete baseball team, maybe this baby boomer can fill in, creaky knees and all, at least for an inning or two.

As always, this is the part where I thank my wife, Vicki, for being with me through all these years of writing. Without her encouragement and support, I doubt if I would have made it this far. She truly is a wonderful wife and I am blessed to have her. Love you, sweetheart!

Prologue

Though baseball is a team game, its character is defined by individual battles: the baserunner testing the arm of an outfielder; the batter laying down the bunt and sprinting to first before the charging infielder or pitcher can throw him out; the runner attempting to steal a base, daring the catcher to peg the ball to second ahead of his flying spikes or, in today's game, his gloved hands.

These moments are thrilling, but the one that catches everybody's eye is the confrontation between the pitcher and batter. It is a classic skirmish between two ballplayers, shutting out the crowd noise and the encouraging shouts of their teammates to focus on the other, just sixty feet away. The struggle begins in the top of the first inning and continues until the last out is made.

Since the game's beginnings in the nineteenth century, countless numbers of these battles have been played out. Two outs in the bottom of the ninth, bases loaded, and the score tied. A pitcher retiring twenty-six straight batters with just one more to go. Game seven of the World Series with everything on the line and your starter ready to pitch on only two days' rest.

On August 16, 1920, there was no pennant at stake quite yet, but it was an important three-game series at the Polo Grounds between the league-leading Cleveland Indians, percentage points ahead of the Chicago White Sox, and the third-place New York Yankees, only a half game back. The Indians were eager to extend their lead, while a New York sweep would push them ahead of the Indians and perhaps the White Sox. Try as they might, neither Cleveland nor New York had finished in first place since the American League began in 1901. The Indians were charter members, while New York had entered in 1903. Each club could boast a superstar, the Indians with player-manager Tris Speaker, the Yankees with the one and only George Herman Ruth.

In the top of the fifth inning with the visitors ahead 3–0, Ray Chapman, experiencing one of his best seasons in the major leagues, led off for Cleveland. A first-class shortstop, considered by some to be the best in the game, he had been in the Cleveland lineup since 1912. A light rain had been falling throughout the afternoon. The baseball was scuffed, moist, and dirty; in those days new balls were only called for when absolutely necessary.

The Yankees pitcher, Carl Mays, in the midst of an exceptional season, stood waiting on the mound. He stared in at the Indians shortstop, trying to get a read on what Chapman might attempt. The right-handed batter crowded the plate, almost leaning into the strike zone. Mays thought he might be trying to bunt his way on, Chapman being one of the elite in the game at dropping one down anywhere between the baselines and using his tremendous speed to beat the throw. If the situation called for it, he could move runners along, topping the American League in sacrifice bunts three times before and was on his way to doing it for a fourth time. Time and time again he bunted the ball in a perfect place, causing nervous fielders to fumble the baseball or throw it into right field. The fans edged forward in their seats, eager to see how the confrontation would play out.

Mays, fearless about moving the hitters back, took his windup and delivered the ball submarine style, his right arm nearly skinning the ground. The ball sped toward home, rising swiftly as it neared the batter's box. Chapman, either losing sight of the ball or completely freezing as it bore in on him, never moved an inch. There was a loud crack and the baseball rolled toward the pitcher's mound. Many of the fans, thinking it was a bunt, started to cheer as Mays scooped up the ball and threw it to Wally Pipp at first. Within seconds the applause stopped and silence ensued. Even the sportswriters in the press box dropped their pencils to observe the sight at home plate. What had they really seen? Chapman did not run to first. Instead, he sank to a sitting position, then slowly crumpled to the ground. The Yankees catcher and the home plate umpire saw blood drizzling from his left ear. Umpire Tommy Connolly hastily took off his mask and turned toward the grandstand, frantically hollering for a doctor. Something terrible had just happened.

A BOY OF MANY TALENTS

The Bible Belt of the United States cuts a wide swathe through the southern states and stretches westward as far as Texas. Its northern point ends in the lower part of Kentucky, where the small city of Beaver Dam sits. Ohio County is home to various small communities, where religion plays a significant role. Going to church on Sundays is a standard event.

In the latter part of the nineteenth century, the area around Beaver Dam was home to Robert Everett Chapman and his wife, Blanche (Johnson). To earn a living wage and take care of a family, a man had two choices there: farming or laboring in the sizable contingent of coal mines. In either option, it meant back-breaking work and a day off on Sunday to don a clean suit and take the family to the local house of worship.

The elder Chapman chose the harsh life of a coal miner, working underground from sunup to sundown. The working conditions were less than poor, with methane gas explosions, collapsing roofs, and falling rocks to deal with on a regular basis. If one survived those hazards, filthy air and a lack of proper ventilation meant lung disease was lurking around the corner. From 1880 through 1923 coal miner deaths in the United States were a staggering 70,000. America needed coal to heat homes and power steam engines; if thousands died in the process of mining it, that was part of the cost. Somehow Mr. Chapman endured relatively unscathed, managing to scrape together enough for a small home, where, on January 15, 1891, a son, Raymond Johnson Chapman, was born. His actual place of birth, as many records, including his World War I draft registration, indicate, was likely McHenry, which lies about three and a half miles southwest of Beaver Dam.

Ray was the second of three children; older brother Roy was born in 1887 and sister Margaret not until 1904. Mom and Dad remembered their younger son as a happy and curious child. At his baptism, Ray surprised his parents by staring wide-eyed at the reverend, not showing any fear throughout the ceremony. Though he would never be overtly religious, Ray carried the Bible given to him that day for all of his adult life.

By the age of three he had developed a penchant for singing, learning several songs and entertaining the neighborhood whether they liked it or not. When the time came he went to school, but in a few years he would be faced with joining his father in the Beaver Dam coal mines.

Neighbors of the Chapmans remembered Ray as a polite, handsome, neatly dressed little boy with black hair and the brownest of eyes. He could be spotted around town, usually munching on a piece of cornbread made specially by his devoted grandma. Summer days were taken up by swimming, picnics with hayrides, and horse racing. In the evenings there was mouthwatering pie and ice cream for the little ones, all they could manage to eat.

Ray was said to be an excellent swimmer as a boy. Stories circulated that he swam across the Ohio River, but details are incomplete about when and where the feat occurred. It may have been a slight exaggeration or more of a legend à la John Henry or Davey Crockett tales. Wintertime brought ice skating over the frozen ponds. When the temperature warmed a few degrees, fishing and hunting were the thing to do. Though life was not always idyllic, growing up in Beaver Dam in the late 1890s represented a slice of genuine Americana, coal mines aside.

Though he had an assortment of tops and marbles to keep him occupied, Ray developed a bad case of baseball fever. He played whenever he could, often with the older boys who frequented the open lots around town. At age ten, Ray did some odd jobs to earn fifteen cents to buy a roll of cotton. He brought the material to his grandmother Johnson, who, under a pledge of secrecy, made him a crude baseball uniform with red piping down the pants. Ray's parents grew suspicious and confronted grandma about her clandestine activities at the sewing machine. She owned up to it, telling her daughter, "It's a baseball suit for Ray. I reckon you're not supposed to know anything about it because you might object."

The Chapmans were not happy with their son's inclination for skipping Sunday church services and heading for the baseball fields, his uniform tucked under his arm. The family observed the Sabbath and disapproved of ballplaying on that day. At times Mr. Chapman followed Ray after church and brought him home, but more often than not the aspiring baseball player eluded him and played all afternoon long. Mrs. Chapman would say years later that the Sunday games were the only time she recalled her son being "naughty."

When Ray was still a growing boy, he made the journey to Owensboro for a summer visit with the Johnsons, his aunt and uncle on his mother's side. The neighborhood boys were putting together a baseball team, the Fourth Street Blues, and recruited Ray to play shortstop. Ray's uncle had played short for the semipro town team some years before, and the boys reasoned that Ray might be predisposed to the position. They certainly had guessed right.

At game time one of the players demanded to play shortstop over Ray. After some discussion, probably because he was an out-of-towner, Ray had to sit out the game. In the home half of the fourth inning the starting shortstop had to leave the game after being hit by a pitch. Ray took his place and showed enough raw ability to earn the starting job. He practiced every day with the Blues, sometimes at vacant lots or behind the local grocery store. Later, against the Snowhill Champions, he slammed his first home run, wowing everybody on the field, including the Snowhill captain, who demanded Ray be banned from the game on the grounds he had way too much skill for a boy his age. The Blues walked off the field, choosing to forfeit rather than play without their star and newfound friend.

This story, recounted years later by the captain of the Fourth Street team, explains how Ray could impact a ball club even at an early age. Even then he showed an easygoing personality, an ability to blend in with his peers. Certainly he had the talent to play with anyone his age or older, but all accounts define him as a friendly, outgoing kid with little ego. Ray had the ability to charm people, making pals without difficulty on and off the baseball field. An endearing smile and a quick story were all he needed to win people over. This engaging characteristic followed him for the rest of his life.

In the early 1900s Mr. Chapman packed up the family and moved west, all the way to Herrin, Illinois, where he purchased a home at 112 South Street. Herrin had about 1,500 people and enjoyed railroad access. The area had a larger number of coal mines that paid better than the ones in Beaver Dam. Brother Roy and his father worked the mines, leaving Ray to attend school so he could learn a skill to keep him from the same fate.

He adapted to the change of scenery, quickly finding friends on the ballfield. Within a few years Ray entered Herrin High School, which held classes on the second floor of an old, worn-out building. The school opened its doors in 1903 with a handful of students and one teacher, the superintendent of Herrin's public schools. The first graduating class in 1906 had a grand total of eight students with an expanded faculty of three teachers.

Ray was probably there from 1905 to 1908, and the one thing we know for sure about his time there was his tendency to skip class and find a place to play ball. Due to the lack of students, the athletic program would not begin until the 1911 school year. If Ray wanted to play football or baseball, he either had to dodge his parents on Sundays or sneak out of school to find a game.

Around this time, Ray met up with another expert ball-player, Bobby Veach. Also a native of Kentucky, Veach moved to Herrin at age seventeen, presumably to work the coal mines with his father. He was three years older than Ray, but the two connected not only as ballplayers but as friends, sharing genial personalities and a sense of humor. In the years ahead they would join forces to play semipro ball in and around Herrin. When both became major leaguers, the baseball field in Herrin would be renamed Chapman-Veach Field.

About a year after high school the five-foot, ten-inch, 170-pound Ray joined the local Stoelzle Hardware team along with Veach. One of the larger businesses in Herrin, Stoelzle Hardware sold tools, farm equipment, and all types of furniture. There was even an undertaker service in the store, discreetly out of view of the general public. With the two rising stars and plenty of funds to back them, the Stoelzle club competed on a high level around the state. In addition to the Herrin team, several newspapers listed Ray as playing for the Mount Vernon, Illinois, semipro club in 1909. "Chatty" (Ray's new nickname, bestowed for all his talking on the field) and Bobby attracted substantial attention from minor league clubs.

Ray's mother was not keen on the idea of her son becoming a professional ballplayer. Like so many other moms of the time, she feared he would turn into a hard-drinking, hard-living man if he left home and associated with older men who had been around saloons and hunted women with less than pure reputations. Mrs. Chapman was a proper woman, unable to look kindly on those who carried vices around with them. Even tobacco chewing was unacceptable, and she was always grilling Ray in the years ahead on whether he might take a chew during the baseball season. She begged him to enroll in college and learn a respectable profession. But as much as she tried, Ray had already determined his future was in pro ball and he had to give it his best shot.

In the fall of 1909, Ray received a contract offer from the Springfield Senators of the Three-I League at a salary of $140 a month. Despite pleas from Mrs. Chapman, he eagerly signed the agreement and dropped it off at the post office. (His friend Bobby Veach signed with another team in the league, the Peoria Distillers.) He spent the winter at home, teasing his mother about meeting up with the seedy characters that hung around the Three-I League ballparks. When the time came for the trip to Springfield, Ray packed his trunk, then called for his mother to check on how well he had arranged his clothes. Mrs. Chapman, peering into his luggage, spotted an antique-looking handgun along with a straight razor. Ray could not resist one last joke on his mom.

Springfield, Illinois, the state capital of the land of Lincoln, sat about 180 miles north of Herrin. It had 51,000 residents and was a major railroad hub. The aptly named Senators ball club competed in a league with more skilled ballplayers than Ray had seen before. Though he had a ton of ability, he lacked polish and the coaching to battle on the same level as his teammates. To win a job, Ray needed to impress his manager. In the exhibition games he played third base, second, and a few times at shortstop while the competition heated up before the start of the regular season.

The nineteen-year-old version of Ray Chapman came with tremendous speed on the bases and an extraordinary throwing arm. A local Springfield paper said, "Chapman has a whip [arm] that enables him to show his worth at the first opportunity." The only problem with the whip was a tendency to pick up a routine ground ball and throw it in the right field stands. Ray made astonishing plays, like dashing behind second base, spearing the ball backhanded, whirling around, and throwing a strike to first base. An inning later he'd grab a one-hopper and throw it five feet over the first baseman's head. His uneven play continued during the preseason, prompting another news story to call him "wild as a March hare."

What kept him on the roster were some outstanding at bats, resulting in doubles, triples and singles with a handful of stolen bases. In a late March game against a picked team—individual players recruited from St. Louis—Ray went 4 for 5 with three singles, a double, and a stolen base while scoring three times. A few games later he had three hits, including a double, in a 6–2 win.

As the regular season approached the Senators mauled Decatur, 12–2. Ray was the batting star, pounding out five hits and stealing twice. This performance probably clinched a place on the final roster. He did not have a set position, playing second, third, or shortstop, but he was at least on the club. However, his spot proved to be precarious at best. Soon newspapers reported that Ray was to be sent to Lincoln of the Illinois-Missouri League, a step down. The move made a lot of sense because of his lack of experience in organized baseball. Playing semipro was one thing, the Tri-State League another.

Nevertheless, a week later he was back in the starting lineup, playing second base against the visiting Waterloo club. Over the next two months, he was in and out of the lineup, struggling as an extra infielder. In early July his batting average sank to .233. Rumors again circulated that Ray's time in Springfield might be over, and on July 25 he was sold to the Davenport Prodigals, another team in the Three-I League, for the sum of $250. In the hazy language of the deal, Springfield retained rights to his services. If for any reason the Senators changed their mind, they reserved the option to buy Ray's contract back at a negotiated price.

The change of scenery appeared to be the right move for the kid from Herrin. Charles "Pa" Shaffer, the Davenport manager, rejoiced at the acquisition, saying, "This Chapman is a cracker-jack, and he will make a good man for us. He is an all-around infielder and should be a promising athlete for our club." A short time later Ray had a great series against his former ball club, slamming a three-run homer well over the outfield fence and glancing off the clubhouse roof.

The big-time hitting did not go unnoticed by Springfield manager Dick Smith. After the series ended, he visited the Davenport team office and demanded Ray be sent back to the Senators. James Hayes, the club's general manager, refused to give up his new talent, telling Smith in no uncertain terms that Chapman was not going anywhere. After several minutes of arguing, Hayes got on the telegraph and wired Springfield owner Dick Kinsella at his ballpark office.

Apparently there was a disconnect between the Senators manager and Kinsella about Ray's status. Smith wanted the player back, while his boss wanted money. Hayes made a cash offer to Kinsella, who quickly wired back, no deal. Several more attempts were made before Kinsella agreed to accept $500 to waive any rights to Ray. With the original $250 already paid, Springfield pocketed $750 to cut ties with Chapman. Not too shabby for a Three-I League ballplayer. In the final analysis, Springfield made a quick cash grab, while Davenport would profit in the long run, on the field and financially.

During his time in Iowa, Ray hosted one of his buddies from Herrin. After the games, the two would go out for dinner, then back to Ray's rooming house. After dinner one night the friend suggested they go out on the town instead and look for girls. Though the easy answer was yes, Ray explained he could not do that as his entire focus was on making his way up to the major leagues. He feared that meeting any women might sidetrack him on his goal. He gave an example of a fellow ballplayer with exceptional talent but started dating a girl and lost his motivation to reach the big leagues. Ray assured his friend this would not happen to him, no matter how good-looking the girls were. The friend was convinced, returning to Herrin to presumably find a woman there.

Ray found a home with Davenport, playing good baseball for the remainder of the season. He ended the year on a high note, going 3 for 4 in a 7–4 win against Rock Island. For the campaign he batted .241 with 87 hits, including 3 home runs. Most impressive were his 23 stolen bases, an indication of things to come. The Prodigals finished in seventh place, with a poor record of 59–80. Still, they drew 57,000 fans for the year, first in the entire league.

Ray left Davenport with the assurance he would be placed on the reserve list for the 1911 season. Each club had the right to exclusively keep a set amount of players on next season's roster. With that he returned to Herrin and his parents' home for some welcome rest and relaxation. Within a day or two the phone began ringing off the hook; calls from friends came with dinner invites and parties to attend. The R & R would have to wait. Ray was Herrin's conquering hero, but still needed to improve his game to compete with the best of the Three-I League. The only way to go was up.

2
THE RUN THROUGH THE MINORS

In the early spring of 1911 a confident and experienced Ray Chapman reported to Davenport for spring training. No longer was he competing for a roster spot. Now he expected to be one of the club's most important assets. Davenport, situated in the southeastern part of Iowa, was laid out on the banks of the Mississippi River. The shipping industry dominated the area, while the Rock Island Railroad served the region, sending a wide variety of products to all sections of the United States. When Ray arrived for the season the growing population stood at 43,000. If for any reason he needed a broom or a package of macaroni, it was no problem because Davenport was the country's leading manufacturer of the two products.

Davenport, despite finishing the 1910 schedule in the second division, still was able to draw a reasonable number of fans to the park. The ownership, with players like Ray, hoped to compete for a pennant. With a winning ball club, there was no telling how many fans would pass through the gates.

The exhibition games got underway in early April. On the eleventh Ray went 2 for 4 while pulling off a spectacular defensive play. With one out and a runner on second, the batter lofted a high fly down the left field line. Ray sped deep into the outfield, caught the ball over his shoulder, then whirled and fired a rope to second base to double off the runner. The crowd gasped at the play, then loudly cheered while the shortstop ran off the field. The papers began to call him "the five hundred dollar beauty" in reference to the cash paid to acquire him the previous year.

Ray was developing into a player that teammates respected and admired. His buoyant personality, accompanied by his ready smile, won over his fellow ballplayers and the Davenport fans. He was the genuine article, playing hard every time out while never failing to compliment others for their play on the field. His constant chatter and exuberance seemed to pick up his ball club whenever needed. Ray's circle of friends increased rapidly due to his genial nature and ability to put people at ease in any circumstance.

A Davenport man who later became a minor league umpire recalled Ray as his favorite ballplayer. As a teenager, the man had the job of selling tickets at the horse gate, where fans drove up their buggies, paid the twenty-five-cent admission fee, and parked the rigs. He said that Ray "was the most immaculate busher [minor leaguer] I ever saw. Above all he always remembered to manicure his fingernails!" Keeping your nails trimmed did not guarantee a spot in the major leagues, but it illustrated how much Ray cared about how he appeared to others.

A sprained ankle put Ray on the sidelines for a week, but he returned in time for a game against the Leland Giants, one of the better African American teams in the Midwest. The visitors from Chicago proved their worth by edging the Prodigals, 2–1.

This being 1911, and racial relations what they were, the Davenport sportswriter wrote, "The poor white trash were wounded and dragged in the dirt at the Prodigal Playground yesterday afternoon when the Leland Giants of Chicago, one of the country's most noted colored combines, outdistanced Dan O'Leary's Caucasians in a 2–1 race riot." The writer went on to degrade the African American women who attended the ballgame, writing that they knew nothing about baseball and stood out with their garish hats and outrageous plumes. Regrettably, this sort of prose was normal and accepted at the time.

The season opened with a four-game homestand against Rock Island. Ray was in one of the cars for the automobile parade to the ballpark, wearing his spanking new uniform of white with maroon trim down the pants. His jersey had a large *D* on the left front, and he wore a white cap with a maroon bill. The socks were white on the bottom and maroon above the ankles. He may have been wearing the team sweater of rich maroon with black trim. When the club went on the road, they switched to blue-gray uniforms with navy trim along with white and navy socks. The caps were white and blue, while the jerseys had "Davenport" across the chest.

Even with the showy uniforms, Davenport dropped the home opener 3–0 to Rock Island, disappointing a crowd of 3,500 to 4,000, paying twenty-five to fifty cents each, that crammed the wooden grandstand. Ray had a quiet game, failing to get a hit in three tries. In all, the team lost five of its first seven games, and lack of hitting and several costly errors by Ray (now being called "Chappie") did not help.

The defeats piled up, but on at least one occasion the Prodigals showed signs of life. Playing Dubuque, Ray was on third base with the bags filled when manager O'Leary flashed the steal sign. The shortstop timed it perfectly, sliding home well before the tag. The other runners advanced too, making the play a rare triple steal. Even with the daring feat, Davenport still was unable to win the ballgame.

Errors on routine plays were still an area of concern for Ray. In a May 19 game against Springfield with two outs and a runner on second, he backpedaled into short left field to grab a high fly ball. He got in position, only to see the ball bounce out his glove, allowing the runner to score. The game went eleven innings before Ray made his third error of the day, letting in the go-ahead run. Reports described him as heartbroken after the game.

As the month of May came to a close, Ray shook off his doldrums. Soon he was hitting with authority, busting out doubles and triples at a clip of almost two per game. If he happened to single, a steal of second base was just about a forgone conclusion. The newspapers took notice, one stating, "Chapman has been playing great ball on this trip. Everybody who has seen him perform during the past week have proclaimed him one of the fastest infielders in the league."

With his batting average approaching .300, Toledo Mud Hens boss Bill Armour traveled to see Ray in action. In the later part of June, he made an offer to the Prodigals for his contract. Speaking for the ball club, Manager O'Leary refused to make the deal. He told the papers, "We couldn't very well let Chappie go at this time. We would be willing to make a deal calling for Chappie's delivery later in the year, but Armour seems to want him right away."

Davenport had been playing much better baseball lately, and the club wanted to take advantage of the now robust attendance filling the cash coffers. Nevertheless, Armour indicated that a journey to Davenport was in the offing to personally negotiate Ray's release. He had the green light from the Mud Hens owner, Charles Somers, who happened to additionally own the American League Cleveland Naps. The two men were looking ahead to Ray joining the Naps as soon as possible, perhaps in a year. No other ball club could attempt to sign Ray once he became a Mud Hen and Somers property.

While the negotiations pressed on, Ray carried on his torrid hitting. In a late June game against Rock Island, he stole three bases then homered in the eighth inning. Statistics published for the first forty games showed him batting .312, with 26 runs scored and 16 steals. On the negative side were his colossal 27 errors. Projecting those numbers over an entire season meant a gaudy number around 90. One could write off the totals to learning on the job, but Ray had a hypercompetitive nature. He reached balls that few shortstops could get to, resulting in him uncorking throws from awkward positions when he would be better served leaving the ball in his glove. More coaching would lessen the unnecessary wild throws and cut down on the errors. Apparently Armour believed he could do just that.

Bill Armour stayed in Davenport for the June 24 Sunday doubleheader against Rock Island, which featured sweltering temperatures and a run on soda pop (sold out by the second game), the Mud Hens owner watched Ray go five for ten, with four of the hits coming in game two. He had many chances in the field and handled them without a miscue. If there was any doubt about signing him, they evaporated in the blistering heat.

When the doubleheader came to a close, reporters crowded around Armour for his thoughts on their shortstop. He said, "I have noticed that he isn't aggressive enough in tagging out runners at second base, but he can soon learn how to turn the trick. He has some other faults which can be easily remedied." Not a ringing endorsement, but reading between the lines indicated that better coaching at a place like Toledo would make Ray a more complete ballplayer.

A few days later photographers from Cleveland arrived to take images of Ray in the field. Hopefully, they did not snap a picture of him throwing a ball into the right field stands and allowing the winning run to score. They must have had inside information, because the announcement that Toledo had reached an agreement with the Prodigals to buy Ray's contract did not come until June 27. The terms were not revealed, but the shortstop would remain in Davenport to the mid-September close of the schedule, then report to the Mud Hens for their last two weeks of the season.

With the signing out of the way, Ray played excellent ball for the balance of his tenure in the Three-I League. In a July contest with Quincy, he belted a long home run along with a double and a single. As the Davenport paper described it, "That great swipe will bring the coming Clevelander a wheelbarrow load of smokin."

Before Ray finished the season he had time to crush a home run over the center field fence and into the river behind the

LOVE AND LOSS

Danville ballpark. Reporters noted that no other player in recent memory had been able to hit a ball at that distance. He was hardly a power hitter, but on occasion he could slam a baseball with the best of them, as the fans in Danville could testify.

September came and along with it the end of Ray's stint as a Davenport Prodigal. In his final game he had three hits and stole three bases in a 6–0 win over Dubuque that lifted his team to the .500 mark. Upon his departure he issued a statement to the press, praising his manager and team. He said, "Dan O'Leary is a star and I hate to leave him. The Boss has certainly been right with me, and I will miss him. I am glad the team made a spurt at the finish, and I am sorry that we didn't get started sooner." With that he packed his suitcase and departed for Milwaukee, where the Mud Hens were playing.

Due to the intimate relationship between the Mud Hens and Naps, the *Cleveland Plain Dealer* ran a feature on Ray going to Toledo. The story highlighted his great attitude, saying he was always the first man out for practice and the first in uniform before each game. He had no apparent bad habits and was a promising candidate for further development.

The sample size would be small, but in sixteen games as a Mud Hen Ray demonstrated what being a promising candidate was all about. He rang up an average of .355 with 22 hits and 8 runs scored. The 1912 campaign promised to be an exciting one, with a young shortstop from Illinois bidding for an opportunity in the major leagues.

3 THE NAPS ARE CALLING

The Toledo club Ray reported to in the spring of 1912 had an abundance of former Cleveland Naps, from stars to non-descript. The standout of the crew was outfielder Elmer Flick, five years removed from his halcyon days as one of the best-performing outfielders in the American League. Cy Falkenberg, a pitcher who had had some success with Cleveland, anchored the staff, while Harry Niles, a one-time Boston and Cleveland outfielder, was counted on to add some punch to the offense. Most of the others had seen time in the major leagues and were hanging on for another season or two until they were cast aside.

Despite facing tougher competition than he had thus far been exposed to, Ray played in a 10–2 loss to Ty Cobb and the Tigers; he had three hits, including a triple. A few days later he had a base hit against Milwaukee while stealing two bases. Once the exhibitions out of the way, it was time to get down to business and start the regular season.

Opening day, April 10, at Swayne Field brought a sellout crowd of 12,928 fans eager to see the new edition of the Mud Hens take on Milwaukee for real. To accommodate them all, the groundskeepers had to use string rope out along the left field line to stack eight hundred fans in foul territory. The pre-game entertainment featured three large combined bands that filled the infield, from the third base line to first. Ray put on a show for the hometown fans, collecting three hits, topped off by a daring feat on the basepaths. In the home half of the eighth inning, with the Mud Hens trailing 5–4, Ray reached base for the third time. With two men out, he was on third. Using his laser-sharp focus, he noticed the Brewers pitcher turning his back to the plate and the catcher looking away while rubbing his leg. Ray took a few steps down the baseline then dashed for home. Those in the crowd who weren't already standing jumped to their feet and roared. Ray scored without a slide, his heady play tying the count at 5–5. Few players had the tenacity to execute a daring play like that. Toledo went on to win, 6–5, while a packed house marveled at the play of their heralded shortstop.

Eleven days later Ray and the Mud Hens faced the Minneapolis Millers and their aging pitcher, former American League great Rube Waddell. In the bottom of the first, Ray scorched a line drive up the middle, knocking in a run and forcing Waddell to duck out of the way. Two innings later he singled to left field, scoring Harry Niles. In the fifth, with runners at second and third, he lined the ball past a drawn-in infield to plate two more runs. In the seventh inning, noticing the Millers third baseman moving back a step, Ray deftly laid down a perfect bunt rolling toward the third base bag for hit number four. At this early juncture in his career, he had already mastered the fine art of bunting. If he noticed the infield playing back, he bunted down the third base line. If only the first and second baseman were a few steps back, he dragged the ball down the first base line, often using his extraordinary speed to beat the pitcher to the bag.

In the home half of the eighth, Ray came to the plate for his final at bat. This time he slammed a line drive to deep left field, bouncing off the scoreboard's wooden uprights. The *News Bee* described him as "chasing around the paths like a hunted deer." He reached third base at full throttle, getting an enthusiastic wave home from third base coach and manager Topsy Hartsel. The relay arrived at the plate just as Ray left his feet for a sideways slide that eluded the catcher's tag. He rose up and dusted off his baggy pants while the crowd gave him an ovation that echoed through northwest Ohio. His performance was one of the greatest ever seen at the Toledo park, one that had fans talking for days. Though it was early in the season, nobody could argue that Ray wasn't primed for a terrific year.

A month into the regular schedule he continued to shine, batting .353 by early May. He hit safely in twenty straight games before finally going hitless on the road at Louisville. Though it was quite early in the campaign, the newspapers began to take up the question of when Charles Somers would be bringing Ray to the Naps. The *Cleveland Leader* posted a photo of the shortstop with the caption "A player of his merit cannot be kept down. Somers owns the Toledo Mud Hens, if he takes Ray, fans in Toledo will scream and attendance could fall. Cleveland needs Ray, Somers is between the devil and the deep blue sea."

Not only were the papers talking about Ray, but many of the American Association team owners were unhappy with Somers's dual ownership. They disapproved of him stocking the Mud Hens with ex–major league players, believing it created an unfair advantage. The owners supposed that if Ray went to the Naps, Somers likely would send the Mud Hens one of short-stops Ivy Olson and Roger Peckinpaugh from the Cleveland roster. Both were struggling with American League pitching but would be as good as any shortstop in the AA. The *Cleveland Plain Dealer* called that argument "drivel," as most major league teams had deals with Association clubs but kept them quiet. Somers was up front about his ownership, putting together an early version of a farm system to sign young ballplayers and keep them in the Cleveland organization. His fellow owners preferred to sign prospects unattached, hoping to find bargains at below-market pricing. This would change, but the Associa-tion owners planned to bring up Somers's combine at the win-ter meetings in an effort to force him to sell out of Toledo.

While the gossip about his future persisted, Ray played the best baseball of his minor league career. By early June he had swiped seventeen bases without being caught. The *Cleveland*

　　　　　　　　　　　　　LOVE AND LOSS

Leader noted that he displayed good judgment when deciding to run, rarely taking ill-advised chances. They quoted statistics that showed runners were caught stealing about 33 percent of the time. So Ray was miles above the curve. When he reached first base and took his lead, pitchers and catchers were acutely aware of what was going to happen but could not stop him.

By the latter part of June the Mud Hens star had 23 steals and 49 runs scored in only fifty-seven games. Not surprisingly, they were sitting in first place. Even so, there were still times when he did show poor judgment. The *Columbus Dispatch* criticized him for trying to go from first to third on a base hit when Toledo was trailing by five runs. This was not smart baserunning, but Ray had a motor that was hard to turn off. The wild heaves into the first base stands still occasionally appeared, but his overall play was the talk of the American Association.

On July 23 Somers was compelled to make a statement to the news outlets. He told them Ray would remain in Toledo to help win the pennant and prop up the attendance figures. The owner was walking a fine line in trying to satisfy fans in two different cities. His Naps were going nowhere despite the presence of superlative hitters in Joe Jackson and Larry Lajoie and a fine season from lefty pitching ace Vean Gregg. Bringing Ray to Cleveland would not make them instant candidates to challenge for first place. For the time being Somers would hold off, but a week later he sent Naps manager Harry Davis to Toledo to see his prized shortstop in action. "Will he or won't he?" became the question for the weeks ahead.

As August rolled around, Somers became annoyed with the attendance numbers out of Toledo. He hinted to the papers that at that pace he might not want to keep Ray with the Mud Hens much longer. The ball club had fallen out of first place and was now trailing Minneapolis by six games. A few days later Somers arrived in Toledo for a meeting with club officials. Though he did not state it publicly, Ray was destined for Cleveland before the month was out. The Mud Hens were on a road trip, a perfect time to buy Ray's contract. With a month and a half left in the American Association schedule, the shortstop already had 45 steals and 93 runs scored to go with a .330 batting average. Nothing was left for him to prove.

The announcement came on August 29 that Ray's contract had been transferred to Cleveland and he would be penciled into the lineup the following day at home against the Chicago White Sox. About a week before, the Naps had brought up first baseman Wheeler "Doc" Johnston from New Orleans. The addition of the two young ballplayers was expected to inject life into the lethargic club and finish the year on a positive note.

In his twelve years as owner of the Naps, Charles Somers had developed a keen eye for talent. Though he had not won any championships, he had brought in loads of gifted ballplayers such as Larry Lajoie, Elmer Flick, Addie Joss, and Bill Bradley, and had traded for Joe Jackson a couple of years earlier when he was an unproven rookie. The one position where he had failed was at shortstop, where a steady parade of bodies had passed through town. Men including Jack Gochnaur, George Perring, and Neal Ball all tried to claim the job, with little success. Terry Turner had the longest tenure at the position but by 1912 had moved to third. When Ray reported to Cleveland, Ivy Olson and Roger Peckinpaugh were the current shortstops on the roster. Somers was not satisfied with the duo, seeing Ray as his answer to the long-standing problem. Ray had all the tools to succeed, giving Somers confidence his decade-long search had come to an end.

For the afternoon game against the White Sox, Ray was batting sixth in the order, one behind Doc Johnston. A good Monday crowd at League Park came through the turnstiles, eager to see what the two newcomers could bring to the table. With a record of 53–69, the Naps had little to play for other than personal statistics. Joe Jackson had a chance for another .400 season, while Lajoie, now in his late thirties, was still one of the feared batsmen in the major leagues.

Though on the downside of his superlative career, Lajoie became an on-field coach for Ray, schooling him on the fine points of playing shortstop in the big leagues. Ray would subsequently credit him as the player he learned the most from. Terry Turner, with the ball club since 1903, started at third base. He could still run, combining with Chapman and Johnston to give Cleveland an exceptionally fast infield, Lajoie not included.

Twenty-one-year-old Steve O'Neill did most of the catching, though his batting needed a lot of development. Veteran Joe Birmingham handled the center field job, flanked by Jack Graney and Jackson, but neither Birmingham nor Graney could hit anywhere near "Shoeless Joe." Overall, the Naps did not have a roster to get anyone overly excited, but with the addition of Ray and Doc Johnston there was now hope for the years to come.

The Chicago pitcher that afternoon was newcomer Phil Douglas, making his major league debut. Douglas would go on to have a tumultuous nine-year career with five different ball clubs before being thrown out permanently by Commissioner Kenesaw Mountain Landis in the early 1920s after he allegedly offered to throw some games.

In the bottom of the first inning the Naps loaded the bases with two out against Douglas. That brought Ray to the plate in his first major league at bat. Though eager to take a swing and drive the ball to the outfield, he remained patient, drawing a walk for the game's first run. Three innings later Johnston led off with a bunt single. Ray dropped a perfect bunt down the first base line and beat the throw to first for a single and the first hit of his Cleveland career. Birmingham then laid down the third consecutive bunt of the inning. Douglas fielded the ball and realized he had no play at first. He looked to second, where Ray had already rounded the bag. Flustered, he threw the ball there anyway, and it sailed into center field, scoring Johnston and sending Ray to third.

On the first pitch to catcher Fred Carisch, Birmingham raced for second. Catcher Ray Schalk fired the ball to third, where Ray was edging down the line, but third baseman Buck Weaver could not reach the errant throw, which bounced into left field. The new Nap jogged home with the second run of the frame. Nothing to it!

The Cleveland fans shouted their approval of the daring baserunning, which had produced two scores without a batted ball leaving the infield. The White Sox were baffled by the tactics, but soon the other American League clubs would be prepared for the baserunning adventures of Chapman and Johnston, making the adjustments to keep it to a minimum. For the day, Chicago could not cope, losing to Cleveland 7–2. Ray's first American League error went virtually unnoticed by the fans.

The next afternoon reality set in, with the Naps on the short end of a 2–1 decision. With the adrenaline still pumping, Ray charged a slow roller and sent his throw sailing into the League Park stands. The error did not lose the game, but it let the Cleveland fans know their new shortstop was a work in progress. In just two weeks he would have seven miscues in his account book.

In addition to the nervous errors, in September Ray got his first look at Walter Johnson's fastball. "Looking" was the key word here, as he fanned three times in four trips to the plate.

In a game played at League Park versus New York, Ray turned into hero and villain at almost the same time. Going into the top of the tenth inning the score was 3–3. The first batter up grounded to shortstop, where Ray fielded the ball but threw low to Doc Johnston for his second error of the game. The runner eventually scored, giving the New Yorkers a one-run advantage heading to the bottom of the tenth.

Leading off the home half of the inning, Ray lined a base hit to right center field. He never slowed down, sprinting to second just ahead of the relay. The throw bounced away from the second baseman and rolled toward the pitcher's mound. Not content with only one extra base, Ray sprang to his feet and raced to third before the bewildered Yankees could react. The Cleveland fans were stunned at the Cobb-like antics, having expected Ray to stop at first with a single. Now he was in scoring position, only ninety feet from home plate. Terry Turner hit safely to right, tying the game at four apiece. A few miscues later, including a passed ball, Turner scored to win the game, sending the fans home buzzing with excitement about Ray's aggressive baserunning.

The addition of Chapman and Johnston gave a wakeup call to an otherwise lackluster baseball team. From September 17 to the end of the schedule, the Naps reeled off thirteen wins in fifteen tries. Their record for September along with the four October games was an outstanding 21–8. Lajoie discovered the fountain of youth, while Jackson pounded the baseball all over the lot. Ray moved up to the second spot in the order and in his short stint with the Naps batted .312.

The last four games of the season were played in St. Louis, with a day off after game two. A one-day trip to Herrin was arranged to play an exhibition game in Ray's hometown, a considerable feat with a train ride of 117 miles each way. The Naps squared off against the locals, then adjourned to the Chapman residence, where a home-cooked meal was served for fifteen hungry ballplayers and family. The entire day's activities spoke well for the newly acquired shortstop, who had clearly made a positive impact on his teammates.

The final statistics for Ray's thirty-one games included an impressive 29 runs scored, almost one per game. The fielding stats were something else. Ray totaled 15 errors, finishing with a fielding percentage of .904. Projected over an entire season, this added up to a colossal 75 blunders or close to 1 every other game. Next year's spring training would mean an intensive program of ground balls and throws to first to work out the problem.

At the end of the St. Louis series, Ray caught a train back for Herrin to spend more time with the Chapmans. Everybody there welcomed him home as a bona fide major league player. Amazingly, he was not the only one, with outfielder Bobby Veach getting a trial with the Detroit Tigers. Both would have long careers in major league baseball, rare for a place tucked away from the big city. Ray stayed in Herrin for a month, leaving in November for his second home, Owensboro, to visit his uncle and aunt along with the growing legion of friends he accumulated there.

While he was in Owensboro, the *Messenger* newspaper chose to write an extended feature on the life of Ray Chapman. They missed the mark on a few items, most notably in stating that Ray was born and raised in Herrin, but for the most part gave an accurate account of his accomplishments to date. It appeared the story had the cooperation of the subject, at least for a good number of the details. It claimed Ray could run the 100-yard dash in 10.25 seconds and the 220 in 23 seconds flat. Who was the best ballplayer in the game? To Ray, it was Ty Cobb, of course, who was a better runner than even Washington's Clyde Milan, who stole a league-leading 88 bases to Cobb's 61. Ray believed Cobb ran for the team, where Milan looked to boost his own numbers. As a gifted base-stealer himself, he knew of what he spoke.

The visit to Owensboro, other than moseying around, included taking part in an indoor baseball league. Played inside an auditorium or an armory, the game featured a huge mush ball, tiny bats, and short distances between the bases. The players wore padding in their uniform pants to allow for diving after the ball or an unexpected spill on the hard floor surface. Ray thought joining in was a smart way of staying in shape and keeping the competitive edge. It was genuine fun, and the fans of Owensboro turned out in large numbers to see him and Mack Allison, a pitcher for the St. Louis Browns.

While still unwinding at the Johnsons' home, Ray decided to take a trip into town to spend a few hours with friends. The horse and buggy were unavailable, having been taken by his uncle. Undeterred, Ray hitched up one of the farm mules and little by little directed him to the city. The ride home was just as slow, and he arrived in the early morning hours. Next time he would not wait for his uncle to claim the buggy.

In late February Ray signed his 1913 contract and left for training camp in Pensacola, Florida. Though he had played well after his 1912 late-season callup from Toledo, it was only a small sample. He still needed to prove he could manage the shortstop job on a season-long basis. In camp were last year's holdovers, Roger Peckinpaugh and Ivy Olson, who had played the majority of games at Ray's position. They were not elite ballplayers ("Peck" would bloom later) but had the experience necessary to make a good showing for the job.

After a few days of running drills, Ray proved to be the fastest man on the squad in the dash from home plate to first base. The papers called him a "keen earnest student" who worked hard every day, showing a lot of pepper in his step and constantly shouting encouragement from his shortstop position. Soon he acquired dear friendships with fellow players Jack Graney and Steve O'Neill that would last the rest of his days. The three often referred to themselves as the "10-11-12's," representing the years they started with Cleveland. Before a tough game or series one of the three would say to the rest of the club, "Don't be worried, 10-11-12 will show 'em."

Ray and Graney became roommates on the road and in Cleveland. When at home they rented space in a three-story home on Hough Avenue, just a couple of blocks from League Park. For roughly $15 per week, they were fed breakfast, lunch, and dinner along with almost half the Naps roster that boarded there. After the 6:00 p.m. feast the boys usually sat on the steps of the front porch, whistling at the attractive girls walking by. At times Ray and Jack would take a young boy who lived at the home to the nearby ice cream shop on Lexington Avenue, where they would buy him a soda. On other nights they would go to the local saloon for a cigar and a beer, usually getting back home by 11:00 p.m.

Ray and Jack both appreciated a good joke and were constantly kidding around at each other's expense. Teammates looking back years later would compare them to popular comedians

Jack Benny and Fred Allen. According to family stories, there were times when the two of them got up in restaurants and clubs to do their own comedy act.

Ray loved to tell anyone that would listen about the origins of Graney's nickname, "Three and Two Jack." Apparently when Graney pitched in the minor leagues he went to a three-and-two count on almost every batter and when hitting always seemed to be facing a three-and-two count himself. How true the story was did not matter; Ray enjoyed teasing his friend whenever he had the chance.

Of course, any friend of Graney's had to be friends with his dog, Larry, the unofficial mascot of the Naps. The little jumping jack excelled in crowd-pleasing tricks and usually traveled with the ball club. When on the road Larry stayed with his two best friends, Graney and Chapman. In the evenings the two would play cards. When Larry needed to go to the bathroom, he would scratch on the door until one of the boys let him out, walk to the elevator barking until somebody let him on, get out at the lobby, and be let out the door, where he took care of business. Then he would repeat the routine to reach his hotel room, where Ray or Jack would open the door and resume their game. Larry was an exceptional dog, to say the least.

Based on his small test from 1912 and how he looked in training camp, Henry Edwards penned a long column in the *Plain Dealer* extolling Ray as the next Honus Wagner. "Here's a prediction," he wrote. "Barring accidents Ray Chapman will make the most sensational debut that was ever accorded to a big league shortstop." Though he thought Ray was as green as a bush leaguer, he compared him to a Ty Cobb or Eddie Collins when they broke into the American League. Edwards claimed that while both players struggled for their first two years, Ray would be a star from opening day and forward. He further stated, "Chapman is a faster man than was either Collins or Cobb and he is a better ball player mechanically than were either of those two great players when they affixed their names to big league contracts." According to the reporter, Ray had a pair of bright batting eyes, an arm of steel, and a keenly working brain.

The article was filled with hyperbole, but Edwards saw a once-in-a-lifetime player in Ray. Comparing him to two of the best players in all of baseball was a bit of a reach, but Edwards had seen them all in his distinguished sportswriting career. The fact he was willing to go out on a limb for a young guy who had yet to play a full season in the majors spoke volumes.

One skill Ray demonstrated during spring training was the ability to hit slow, sweeping curveballs. Many ballplayers could only wave at the roundhouse offerings, but Ray had the ability to reach for the ball, slapping it to the opposite field. In his last season in the American Association, pitchers stopped throwing him the roundhouse curve and tried other methods to get him out.

Near the end of March, Ray distanced himself from the competition at shortstop, closing in on the starting job. Manager Birmingham hinted at such, chatting with reporters about other teams' shortstops. "They can talk about their short field wonders, but I think we have a mighty good little shortstop ourselves. Give that boy [Ray] another year in the big leagues and he won't have to take his hat off to any of them."

In an intersquad game Ray showed off his baserunning skills to all present. He beat out an infield roller for a base hit, then stole second and third. On another slow grounder he dashed for the plate, scoring without a throw. His foot speed and know-how were an indication of things to come in the years ahead. Now Peckinpaugh chased fly balls in the outfield, and Olson, more of a jack-of-all-trades, took grounders at third and second. Starting at shortstop was Ray Chapman.

On April 11 the Naps opened the 1913 season at home against the Chicago White Sox. Though it was a blustery day with temperatures near the freezing mark, over 15,000 fans made their way to the ballpark. Usually spectators could be seen perched on the nearby rooftops, but due to the weather the building tops were empty. A lone fan climbed a telephone pole on Lexington Avenue and gamely held on despite the swirling winds around the park.

Even with the harsh weather, a local doctor commented on the benefits of being outdoors after a long and chilly winter and enjoying a baseball game. "The game is a fine thing. I have only one fault to find with it—there is too much spitting among the players." With most of the players chewing tobacco, gum, or licorice, the spewing was inevitable.

The Naps took the field with Ray at shortstop, batting second. Doc Johnston led off, Ivy Olson batted third, Jackson batted fourth, and Lajoie batted fifth. Joe Birmingham, now player-manager, Jack Graney, and catcher Grover Land made up the bottom of the order. Vean Gregg did the pitching and was in command throughout the 3–1 victory. Ray had a base hit in three at bats but booted a ground ball for an error.

The miscues peaked against St. Louis when Ray committed three errors in a 6–2 win. In past years Cleveland fans would have been booing at the loudest levels, but this time they shouted encouragement to their beleaguered shortstop. When he picked up a ground ball and threw cleanly to first, the fans gave him a rousing cheer, which led to Ray taking off his cap and bowing his head. After the game he told reporters, "Every spring I have two or three bad games. Had the fans got after me today, I don't know where I would have thrown the ball." It seemed the folks in the grandstand had taken a liking to Ray for his constant hustle and heads-up baserunning. Whether he was stealing a base or zipping from first to third on a base hit, the fans sensed there was something special about the way he played baseball. They were willing to stay with him, at least for now.

A week or two later Ray began to find himself, both on offense and defense. In a win against New York he handled several line smashes flawlessly while stroking two singles and laying down two sacrifices. His ability to get his bat on the ball and move runners from first to second started to take shape. With a dead ball and fences too far for most hitters to reach, the art of sacrificing runners to second paid dividends. Ideally a team's leadoff man had a knack for getting on base while the second hitter's job was to move him along. Ray fit into that slot with an uncanny talent for making contact and pushing the baseball far enough for the runner to advance safely. He did this over and over again, quickly making him one of the best at it in the American League. Not glamorous like a long triple or inside-the-park home run, but still a much needed weapon for a team looking to score one run at a time.

On Friday, May 16, the Naps were hosting the Athletics. With a good crowd on hand, the Naps were down 5–4 through six innings. In the bottom of the seventh Doc Johnston led off with a base hit, followed by Ray's double, Johnston stopping at third. With the A's infielders moving in to cut off a run at the plate in the event of a playable ground ball, Ivy Olson slashed a drive at shortstop Jack Barry, who got a glove on the baseball but could not keep it in front of him. Ray tore for third, while Johnston started for home, thought better of it, and scampered back for third. With Ray standing on the bag, Doc had no choice but to reverse himself and run toward home, where the A's trapped him in a rundown. Seeing his teammate in trouble, Ray sprinted back to second, only to find Olson a few feet from the bag. They both froze while Johnston was tagged out and a lightning relay to second retired Olson. Standing in no-man's land, Ray dug in his spikes attempting to reach third. He didn't make it, and the A's completed a most unorthodox triple play, a real embarrassment for all three Cleveland players. Among them they totaled two singles and a double but had nothing to show for it. For the game Ray had four hits with two RBIs, but the shoddy baserunning overshadowed his performance and helped produce a disappointing loss for the Naps.

Over a decade later, famed sportswriter Ring Lardner would recall the triple play in his syndicated column. Using his profound sense of humor and sarcasm, he did a play-by-play of the incident, calling out Ray and his two partners in crime for their baserunning gaffes. Readers no doubt laughed wholeheartedly at the story, though the Cleveland fans likely grimaced while drinking their coffee or tea.

The month of May came with a lot of anticipation at League Park. Boston, the reigning champions, came to town for a series with the Naps. There was talk of the Red Sox being irked at the locals for beating them eleven times the previous season. The game soon turned into a rugby scrum, with the Boston players employing some unsavory tactics.

In the Naps' second inning, Jack Graney was standing on third when catcher Bill Carrigan walked toward the mound to speak with pitcher Dutch Leonard. Graney realized the catcher had failed to call time out and made a dash to the plate. Racing to meet him, Carrigan, without the ball, slammed headlong into the Cleveland outfielder, knocking him unconscious. Dutch Leonard tagged Graney, and the umpire, ignoring Carrigan's dirty tactic, raised his right arm to signal the out. Understandably, the Cleveland players were furious, but the call stood. After a moment, Graney came to, stood up, shook off the cobwebs, and stayed in the game.

In the top of the fourth, Joe Jackson attempted to score on a squeeze play. He came in spikes flying at Carrigan but was tagged out and took a hard knee in return from the catcher. The rest of the contest saw spike wounds back and forth. Lajoie would later complain about a painful bloody foot in a jarring collision at first base.

After the game, which the Naps won, both teams headed for the tunnel to the locker rooms, where a nasty brawl took place with at least twelve of the ballplayers throwing punches. After the fighters were separated, the Boston players said they were going to "get" the Cleveland infielders during the upcoming June series at Fenway Park. Why Ray and the others were a target remains a mystery, but when the Naps arrived at Fenway

　　　　　　　　　　　　LOVE AND LOSS

Park, Ray, Johnston, Lajoie, and Ivy Olson were wearing shin guards as a precaution.

The first two games went without incident, and Ray, believing the hostilities were done with, removed his shin guards before game three. In the visitor's half of the eighth, with the score deadlocked at five apiece, he reached third base with less than two outs. He edged down the line, measured the pitcher, then took off for home. As he slid Carrigan put on the tag then stomped forcefully on Ray's leg with his spikes, causing a nasty four-inch cut, clear through to the shinbone. Blood poured out in two places, a repulsive exhibition of Carrigan's awful actions. Sure, spiking was part of the game, but the Boston catcher went out of his way to apply the heavy foot to Chapman's leg.

Ray had to leave the game to take a seat on the bench while the Cleveland trainer attempted to stop the bleeding and clean the wound. Teammates noted the blood gushing all over the white part of Ray's sock. The guys were already on edge going back to the third inning when Boston's Joe Wood unloaded a fastball that struck Lajoie square on the wrist. The great one approached the mound, challenging the pitcher to meet him there. Wood turned his back and walked behind the rubber, choosing to stay silent. Without any further mishaps, the tie game continued for fifteen innings, with the Naps pulling out the victory, 9–5. True to the Deadball Era, Cleveland pitcher Vean Gregg went the entire fifteen innings, while Red Sox relief hurler Dutch Leonard threw the final nine.

Manager Birmingham blasted the Red Sox tactics after the game, telling reporters, "Boston started this rough stuff at Cleveland and gave us a bad name all over the country. Now the public itself can see who is to blame." The spike wound would keep Ray inactive for sixteen days.

Upon his return to the lineup, Ray found himself in the middle of a controversy. Manager Birmingham liked the way Terry Turner had filled in at shortstop over the last two weeks. Rather than asking him to take a seat on the bench,

Birmingham shifted Turner to second base and removed Lajoie from the lineup. His reasoning was that Turner played much better defense and worked smoothly with Ray. Lajoie still had a potent bat, but in his eighteenth season did not cover much ground at second.

The decision sent Lajoie into a rage, threatening to quit the team and leave Cleveland for good. Birmingham had a point on keeping the defense sharp, but how do you bench a superstar and not get hammered for it? It's unknown if owner Somers intervened, but soon Lajoie was back in the lineup for the remainder of the season. The double play combo of Chapman and Lajoie needed some fine-tuning, eventually becoming above average, but the Naps played winning baseball despite Ray's learning on the job and Lajoie's inability to cover ground as he did years earlier.

By August, Ray's leg had completely healed, as evidenced by some tremendous displays of speed on the bases. At Washington he drove a line drive over center fielder Clyde Milan's head. The fans rose to their feet, watching two of the fastest men in baseball race in opposite directions. Ray sped around third base and scored standing for an inside-the-park home run. A week later he did the same in Cleveland, slamming a drive to dead center field and flying around the bases with two Nap runners ahead of him. The three-run homer clinched a 10–1 romp over Philadelphia.

At the end of the month in St. Louis, Ray clobbered a ball to the deepest part of Sportsman's Park, a distance of 422 feet, and raced around the bases before the ball was thrown back to the infield. Friends from Herrin arrived a day too late for the home run, but still got their money's worth the following day. Close to two hundred of Ray's best friends saw him collect two hits while scoring three runs in a 9–1 win, marking a three-game sweep of the Browns.

On September 7 the Naps were in Detroit for a Sunday game at Navin Field. In the first inning Ray belted another liner to center, this time over Ty Cobb's head. Once again two of the swiftest men in baseball leaped into action. Cobb sped to the deepest part of the field, recovered the ball, turned, and threw a perfect relay to cutoff man Oscar Vitt in short center field. Vitt made the pivot as Ray tore around third base, Birmingham waving him on. The throw to catcher Red McKee was right on target, giving him an instant to glove the ball and block the plate. Ray came tearing in, lowered his shoulder, and crashed into the Tigers catcher, knocking the ball out of his grasp. For all his effort the official scorer called the hit a triple and safe at home with an error charged to McKee. Physical contact at home plate was more than okay at the time, with neither the runner nor the catcher asking for or giving any quarter. Ray had mastered several different types of elusive slides but chose to go the hard way to make the run count. The Naps won the game 6–4.

The season ended well for Cleveland, as they finished third with a fine record of 86–66. Strong pitching from Vean Gregg and Cy Falkenberg (now back in Cleveland) paved the way along with Jackson and Lajoie's timely hitting. Despite Henry Edwards's lofty prediction, in his first full season Ray finished with a so-so batting average of .258, 78 runs scored, and 29 steals. His 48 errors were third most in the league. Even so, he would be named to several All-American teams compiled by sportswriters around the country. Throughout the year he demonstrated a flair for spectacular plays, leading many writers to believe stardom was just around the corner. The bar had been raised for the 1914 season, and the Naps expected their shortstop to take a leap forward to prove he belonged among the best.

4
A BAD BREAK

Instead of unwinding at home, Ray spent most of the off-season in Owensboro working for his uncle, J. R. Johnson. For $8 a day he fed and cleaned the stalls for two hundred cows and one hundred hogs. Maybe he believed the heavy workload would keep him in shape, or maybe the money was worth the effort. Regardless, he toiled for three months, arriving in Herrin in mid-January with about $500 in his pocket. The *Plain Dealer* contacted him, wanting to get an idea of what he had done in his time away from the ballfield. Ray told the paper, "I was never so happy to get home before. If you have ever acted as a chambermaid for cows and hogs you can appreciate how glad I am to get where I can sleep without the alarm clock routing me out of bed at 4:30 a.m." He claimed to be in great condition from tossing around a few tons of hay daily. Not quite baseballs but using the throwing arm, nevertheless.

In late January, Bill Phillips, manager of the new Federal League Indianapolis Hoosiers, came calling. The Federal League, with several strong moneymen behind it, had declared itself a major league in direct competition with the National and American Leagues. They planned to lure away players like Ray with large salary increases over what they had been earning. It was a gamble, but ballplayers now had the rare opportunity to play one side against the other.

Charles Somers anticipated the tactic, sending a wire to Herrin instructing Ray to come to Cleveland ASAP. Later in spring training Ray would give his version of events. "I felt like I was done when I received the telegram from the secretary to come to Cleveland at once. Now I realize it was pretty soft for me." When he arrived at the Cleveland train station he was startled that the Naps team official kept calling him Mr. Chapman instead of Ray or Chappie. Usually only the manager of the ball club was called "Mr."

Upon reaching the League Park offices, Ray was further taken aback when Charles Somers had a contract for him and asked Ray how much he wanted on the dotted line. "I had planned to put in a bid for a $1300 raise," Ray recounted. "But I almost lost the strength in my fingers when I did it and signed the contract." In his four years of trying to negotiate his services, Ray had never had a team owner agree to his demands without any bargaining. Being relatively young, he did not fully understand the opportunities made available by the emergence of the Federal League. Although he was elated with the raise, afterwards he would realize he could have haggled for more money, probably in the $2,000 range.

Most team owners, intent on keeping their core players, grudgingly followed suit, shelling out considerable sums to keep at least their star players happy. Tris Speaker was reported to be receiving a $12,000 contract from Boston, while Ty Cobb was said to be agreeing to a two-year deal at $18,000 per season. As for Ray, he was delighted with the money, ending his slightly embellished story by saying, "I wouldn't have traded places with the President of the United States!"

The 1914 Naps training camp took place in Athens, Georgia. Ray reported on time, eager to improve his play of the previous season, particularly his inclination for wild throws and ground balls through his legs. He worked hard on all aspects of his game, including sliding. Though already adept at stealing bases, he wanted to broaden his technique for avoiding the second basemen or shortstops attempting to put on the tag.

A few days into camp, Ray was delivered a hefty package containing two new bats turned for him by the same gentleman who manufactured bats for Honus Wagner. It seems that throughout the 1913 season Ray could not find a bat he liked enough to use every day. While on an eastern road trip, he learned that the man who made bats for Wagner lived in Scranton, Pennsylvania. On a day off, Ray boarded a train for Scranton to meet with the bat maker. They agreed on specifications and that the bats would be delivered the following March. He promised his teammates that with the new sticks in hand, batting .300 for the 1914 season was a done deal.

On March 12 the Naps went through a listless morning practice. Observing some of his players limping around, still tender from the last few workouts, manager Birmingham decided to suspend practice at noon for fear of one of his aching players getting injured. With only minutes remaining on the clock, Ray decided to try out a few slides then call it quits for the day. As he slid into third base, his spikes caught the firm turf in front of the bag. He lay with his right leg extended in a grotesque manner, turning side to side in pain while his teammates circled around him trying their best to help. After several minutes they gently carried him to the grandstand. A car was called and they loaded Ray into the back seat for the short ride to the team hotel, where a local doctor was summoned. The preliminary diagnosis was a fractured ankle, but the doctor suggested X-rays the following morning at the University of Georgia.

While Ray lingered in bed, visitors came by every hour to look in on their injured teammate. Jack Graney stopped by with Larry the dog. After a moment the little guy jumped onto the bed and thoughtfully snuggled next to his wounded friend. Larry had amazing empathy, knowing that Ray was hurting and needed help. The faithful dog stayed in the bed the remainder of the day (bathroom breaks excluded) and through the morning until the automobile came to take Ray to the hospital for his X-rays.

The results were inconclusive, but the doctors believed the ankle had been fractured. Joe Birmingham elected to get another opinion, driving Ray to Atlanta, where he literally hopped on a train for Cleveland to consult with the team physician, Dr. Morrison Castle. Before the trip a shaken Birmingham told sportswriters about Ray, "His whole heart and soul are wrapped up in baseball. He worries over things that go wrong, worries himself sick at times. I've never seen another like him."

Ray's injury sparked a debate in the newspapers about the newfound use of sliding pits, elongated ditches filled with manicured soft sand. Many felt players should not slide into bases during spring training but use the pits. Teams such as the New York Giants who used them claimed leg injuries were at a minimum. Certainly, the Naps organization became acutely aware of the alternative.

The Naps manager knew that without Ray in the lineup, the team's chances of building on last year's third-place finish were cloudy at best. They had two of the best hitters in the game in Lajoie and Jackson, but missing their shortstop poised for a breakthrough season put a damper on their plans. Not only was he their best baserunner and stealing threat, but they would miss having Ray to sprint into left field to snare popups or gallop behind second to lasso a sharp grounder and toss the batter out. Birmingham's best alternatives to fill in were Terry Turner and Ivy Olson.

As might be expected, Ray did not take the accident as part of the job. He had been playing organized baseball since before high school and had never been out of the lineup for an extended period of time. He was still twenty-three-years old, approaching his second full season of major league baseball. Being sidelined for an indefinite period was too much for him to accept. Ray told reporters, "I wouldn't feel so bad if I had been loafing. If I were one of those fellows who simply play for the money. But I tell you it's tough to be laid up this way when a fellow is crazy about baseball."

Ray, as others did, played the game for the thrill of competition. In Cleveland, fans were quick to notice him as the first one out of the dugout to slap the back of a teammate for a timely hit or smart baserunning. His boyish spirit along with his never-give-up attitude rarely slowed down, and he always played as hard as possible, whether the score was 2–1 or 12–0. Stealing a base when you have a commanding lead in the eighth inning might provoke ire from the opposition, but in Ray's case he was simply playing ball as he knew it. Being sidelined was not part of his makeup.

The day after the mishap, Ray arrived in downtown Cleveland, where Dr. Castle was waiting at the train station to take his patient to nearby Charity Hospital for X-rays. The far better equipment there clearly showed two broken bones, a spiral fracture of the fibula and a transverse break of the tibia. Dr. Castle estimated a likely return to action in early July. Ray was to remain at the hospital for at least a month with little or no walking, then a light workout schedule for May. If the leg responded he could begin practicing with the team on a strictly limited basis.

Extended hospital stays can be tortuous for anyone, particularly those who are in constant motion. Ray had little choice but to remain in bed, tossing oranges in the air and catching them, while he was convalescing. To boost his spirits, Charles Somers and several other Naps sent daily boxes of candy to their fallen teammate. Ray was described as "a fiend for sweet meats." Estimates were given that he devoured an implausible seventeen pounds of chocolate during his recovery.

While still confined, Ray got word of a new patient admitted for a sprained ankle. Catcher Steve O'Neill arrived at Charity for a short stay. It was an opportunity for the two close friends to visit one another. Neither could get around well but managed to spend hours catching up on the latest baseball news from the Naps and the American League.

For the most part Ray managed to be a model patient, but in early April he snuck out of the hospital on crutches to watch a hockey game between the Cleveland Athletic Club and the Montreal Stars. Later in the month doctors removed the heavy cast and took numerous X-rays of the ankle. Dr. Castle was relieved to see the bones fusing together, an encouraging sign of a full recovery. Within moments, Ray happily bent his ankle and wiggled his toes, the first time since the accident. He even walked a short distance without any help, another sign he was on the mend.

A few weeks later he arrived on crutches at League Park, donning his uniform to pose with his teammates for a group photo. On May 5 he got approval to travel with the team, taking part in modified infield practice under the direction of Birmingham and the team trainer. Each day his mobility increased while his favoring of his right leg became less pronounced. On May 17 a self-assured Ray told reporters, "I count on making my appearance in the game again, Manager Birmingham willing, on June 15. I think I will be as strong and fast as ever by that time."

One innovative way of strengthening the leg involved a player piano. For a short length of time he pumped the pedals daily with his foot, trying to regain the lost muscle power. This was a unique method of therapy, but not appropriate for anybody within hearing range of the keyboard.

His confidence in an early return was a great encouragement to the ball club, which had been floundering. As of May 16 the Naps had a dismal record of 8–17, with key players aside from Ray in and out of the lineup. Lajoie, Jackson, and the already mentioned Steve O'Neill spent time on the bench, while three-time twenty-game-winner Vean Gregg developed a sore arm, which crippled the mediocre pitching staff.

While in the later stages of his recovery, rumors circulated that Ray had been approached again by representatives of the Federal League. He quickly put an end to the speculation by saying, "I would be foolish to jump. The Naps have taken care of me while I have been out with a broken ankle. It is up to me to stick by them when I am able to play." Probably the nonstop amount of free chocolate had something to do with it.

A Ray (Chapman) of hope appeared on June 16, his third game back, when he jogged out to his shortstop position to face Washington. In the second inning he singled and was on second when pitcher Bill Steen lined a base hit. Ray streaked around third, hustling for home. The throw was on line, causing him to instinctively leave his feet and slide for the plate. While the entire Naps bench held their collective breath, Ray bounced up, an ear-to-ear smile on his face and a run scored. Buoyed by Ray's return, Cleveland won six out of seven games. However, reality set in with the losses piling up at an ungodly rate. Near season's end, the Naps were firmly in last place, destined for a win-loss total of 51–102, 48 games out of first and a distant 18 games behind the seventh-place Yankees.

Their last two games at League Park were with the Chicago White Sox. The always exuberant Ray played with a little too much intensity. Though nothing was at stake, in the first game he got into a shouting match with Chicago's second baseman, Lena Blackburne. Players had to step between them. The next day Ray had words with the Sox's Jacques Fournier, and only quick action by new second baseman Bill Wambsganss stopped the two from throwing punches. Incidentally, the Naps' new infielder would have his name shortened to Wamby in the box scores, as the ten letters were too long to squeeze in. The Cleveland players had taken to calling him Wamby shortly after his acquisition—hence the name Wambsganss disappeared on both counts.

Ray may have been frustrated by the Naps' poor showing and his extended absence. His emotions got the best of him, leading to a couple of near fights on two successive days. Until that time he had been described as a gentleman, always respectful to the umpires and his teammates. Apparently there was a degree of anger brewing inside, which came to the surface at

LOVE AND LOSS

season's end. Fighting in baseball did not raise any eyebrows, but coming from Ray the ungentlemanly behavior was more than a little surprising.

Ray struggled at the plate for much of the season but by the end was able to raise his batting average to .275, with 103 hits, including 10 triples, and 24 steals. His fielding did not follow suit, with 42 errors in 106 ballgames. After every stellar play in the field, it seemed a miscue would follow. The breakthrough season had not taken place, but the upside was still there to be tapped.

After missing the first two months of the season, Ray looked to continue playing baseball when and where he could. In the fall an invitation arrived from Frank Bancroft, longtime business manager of the Cincinnati Reds, asking Ray to join an American League All-Star team in a barnstorming tour across the United States from the middle of October through November and possibly December. Ray would play shortstop against the National League All-Stars. The big selling point was a two-week trip to Hawaii, where eight games would be scheduled along with days off to sightsee in a magical paradise.

In the early 1900s barnstorming was a means for ballplayers to earn extra money over the fall and winter months plus gain some goodwill for the game. The promoters of the tours, such as Bancroft, fronted part of the money for train travel, hotels, and other expenses. Once the games started, they received shares of the gate receipts. A proper tour scheduled in the right cities without any rainouts usually meant a return for both parties along with an opportunity to see much of the country. The sixty-eight-year-old Bancroft had the necessary experience with barnstorming, starting with a player tour of Cuba way back in 1879 and going forward with additional trips over a number of years. He appeared to be the man to pull off a successful tour.

Not everyone was a fan of postseason tours. More than a few major league owners frowned on them, believing their players earned ample money during the regular season. If a player earned a fairly large sum barnstorming, he might feel he could comfortably hold out while trying to negotiate a better contract for the upcoming year. The owners also stewed about potential November or December injuries that might carry over into the season.

Ray accepted his invitation and arrived in Milwaukee on October 17 for the opening game of the tour. The Americans lineup featured Ray's teammate, pitcher Willie Mitchell, along with Joe Bush of the Athletics doing much of the hurling, as well as outfielder Duffy Lewis from Boston, George Moriarty of the Tigers at third, Washington's John Henry, a future close friend, doing the catching, and another Red Sock, "Doc" Hoblitzell, at first. With his playing days just about over, catcher Ira Thomas of the Philadelphia Athletics served as team manager.

The Nationals had the Phillies' Grover Cleveland Alexander and Boston's Bill James pitching along with New York's Jeff Tesreau. The outfield had the Pirates' Max Carey and the Cardinals' "Cozy" Dolan, Bill Killefer from the Phillies catching, and Fred Snodgrass, Artie Fletcher, and George Burns from the Giants. The rosters would be completely filled out by the start of the tour.

On the eve of game one, the American League players huddled together to talk about the Boston Braves and their World Series sweep over the Athletics. Wanting some payback, Ray and the others decided to play as hard as possible to teach the Nationals a lesson. They won the first three games, exasperating the Nationals and starting bad feelings between the teams. Before long the two squads were staying at different hotels and no longer socializing.

The tour continued west, stopping in several out-of-the-way places, including Potlatch, Idaho, and Mandan, North Dakota. Frank Bancroft counted on the allure of major league baseball to these small communities and was rewarded with sold-out crowds of up to 5,000 fans, most of whom had never seen big leaguers in action. In Walla Walla, Washington, the gate receipts were listed at $2,378, the All-Stars taking with them $1,057. With over forty games scheduled plus decent weather, there was sure money to be made.

On November 1 the two teams squared off in Portland, Oregon. In the top of the fifth inning Max Carey scorched a line drive, headed for left center field. At the last instant Ray made a tremendous leap, seemingly several feet above the ground, while spearing the ball one-handed. The fans were astonished, rising to their feet and applauding for several minutes. The Americans lost the game 3–2, but the newspapers were filled with accounts of Ray's sensational play. Writers were now calling him "Chappy" or "Chappie," completely won over by his unceasing hustle and never-give-up style of play.

Six days later in San Francisco, Ray hit his stride, going 4 for 5 and driving in a pair of runs. Word had spread throughout California that both teams were playing with a vendetta as opposed to taking an extended vacation. This type of play motivated fans to turn out and see for themselves, triggering a significant spike in attendance. Crowds of up to 8,000 fans were greeting the players all along the West Coast cities. With hotel and travel costs paid up, each player was in line to receive $800, with the highly anticipated Hawaii tour still to come.

The traveling party numbered forty-six, including thirteen wives of the players. Some of the superstitious ones in the tour feared a "hoodoo," or jinx, because of the unlucky number. A few days later Jimmy Miller, one of the Nationals reserves, announced plans to transport his fiancée to San Francisco and marry before sailing to Hawaii. The new bride raised the total to fourteen wives, canceling out the fearsome hoodoo.

During the last week of November, the tour left San Francisco for the six-day trip across the Pacific Ocean aboard the steamship *Manoa*. They arrived in Honolulu on Tuesday, December 1, with games beginning on the third. They were the first major league teams to visit Hawaii since Albert Spalding's world tour of 1888. Unfortunately, Spalding's group landed on a Sunday, only to find out no baseball was allowed on that day. Spalding and company spent the night and set sail the next day for Australia.

Ray and his teammates were greeted at the large harbor by thousands of Hawaiians eager to welcome the honored guests. The players were taken by automobile to the Young Hotel. At a formal luncheon the following day, a crowd of 350 people jammed the sixth-floor banquet hall, forcing extra tables to be set up in the hallway. After the luncheon, the players changed clothes and dashed to the gorgeous white-sand beaches for an afternoon of swimming and sunbathing. Not surprisingly, Ray would later comment that Hawaii was the trip of a lifetime.

In the first three games played, Ray batted .444 with four hits in nine tries. He quickly won over the islanders, but this time it was in his off-field behavior where he made his mark. A group of players agreed to attend an evening benefit for the YMCA on December 5. The morning and afternoon were set aside for sightseeing, including a visit to an active volcano in Hilo, and by evening time one by one the players begged off on the dinner. In the end only Ray and Ira Thomas attended.

The hundred people who paid for the evening were disappointed, but after dinner Thomas stood up to give a lengthy talk about his days with the Philadelphia Athletics and Connie Mack. He fielded questions about Eddie Collins, Charles "Chief" Bender, and other famous A's, then sat down to a huge round of applause. Though not scheduled to speak, Ray walked to the podium, his ever-present smile flashing. He told the crowd that Thomas had covered much of the ground, but he would try to entertain them for a few minutes.

He spoke of his days in Herrin and how he managed to get to the Three-I League and then to Toledo and Cleveland. He talked earnestly about how a ballplayer needed to follow a clean lifestyle off the diamond while using his head when on the field. He said, "All great ballplayers love the game and wouldn't give it up even if their living didn't depend on it." He went on to say, "In baseball there is always something to learn.

At the end of every season a player can stop and think over all he didn't know when the season started."

Ray told several baseball stories, then took questions from the enthusiastic audience. He was asked what he thought about visiting a nearby fort where a huge cannon was demonstrated. He remarked, "When they shot off that fourteen inch gun at Fort Derussy the other night, I thought right away of Walter Johnson pitching." After much laughter, he walked through the crowd, shaking hands with all the attendees. As the only full-time player willing to give up his free time, Ray gained much attention that evening and the next morning when the local newspapers came out. One of the papers summed up the evening by stating, "It is easy to understand why Chapman is one of the most popular and one of the most valuable of the Cleveland club."

For the remainder of the stay, "Chappie" Chapman drew much attention. Friday's game was a win for the Americans, 12–6. In front of an overflow crowd at Moiliili Park, Ray lined a single to right field. Knowing pitcher Grover Cleveland Alexander was substituting as the right fielder, he rounded first and sped for second, daring "Alex" to throw him out. A hurried throw was not in time to catch Ray, who showed the fans an example of smart baserunning.

On Monday another large crowd filled the grandstand. To the delight of the fans, who were eager to see a genuine home run, it was Chappie who walloped a drive over the center field wall that landed on a small greenhouse outside the grounds. Ray could do nothing wrong that day, making several difficult stops and throwing out the runners. Once again the local papers offered their praise, writing about his "fast and tricky fielding."

The successful tour ended on December 13 with the Americans winning in a breeze, 9–1. In the sixth inning Ray lined a shot into the right field corner. He steamed around third base and bluffed a dash for home. The wary relay man heaved the ball to the plate far enough off line to allow Chappie to score standing up. It was his last gift to the appreciative fans.

Three days later the traveling party bid farewell, boarding the *Manoa* for the cruise to San Francisco. The players waved goodbye, their wallets filled with an additional $700 each. Taking into account the heavy expenses for steamship tickets along with first-class hotels, the expedition proved to be a rousing success. On the road for two months, visiting approximately forty different cities and covering thousands of land and sea miles, Frank Bancroft undoubtedly brought home a winner. Even if the tour had only broken even, all the participants got their money's worth, playing baseball and visiting some of the most beautiful islands in the world.

While the players were sailing back to San Francisco, the National League owners voted to abolish barnstorming, citing as their reason poor teams traveling the country and causing embarrassment to the high standards of major league baseball. The American League owners were expected to meet soon and follow the Nationals' lead. It is curious how the owners came to their far-reaching decision. Were they not following the newspaper articles about Bancroft's venture, or were they closely reading every word, appalled at the players' good fortune? Were they resentful of all the participants making money and traveling to Hawaii without their even receiving a piece of the action? Given the owners' stranglehold on the ballplayers during the regular season, it makes sense they could not stomach the idea of the guys making decent money outside of their control. The traveling party went home with cash in their pockets and great stories to tell without the benevolence of their bosses.

In late December, Ray arrived in Herrin, ready to decompress for the next two months. In addition to the money, he had received a gold cigarette case during the course of his travels. For his mother he brought home six exquisite carved brass finger bowls from the islands, and a ukulele with an instruction book for his sister, Margaret. The youngest member of the Chapman family possessed musical ability, probably more so than her brother. At one point Ray offered his sister an opportunity to attend the Juilliard School of Music after she graduated high school. He would pay her tuition and all expenses, but circumstances ended up dashing her chances.

Ray hardly ever came home to Herrin without gifts for his family. Margaret recalled that on one occasion after the baseball season he brought home a cat for her to take care of. When Ray traveled with the ball club to the eastern cities, including Boston and New York, he bought his sister shoes and dresses, and on one occasion a chic winter coat, at the trendy women's clothing stores. She would later note feeling somewhat self-conscious wearing the clothes around Herrin because no other women in town had anything like them.

When time permitted, he would take his younger sister to Chicago to buy clothes. Acting like a caring parent, Ray would often tell his mother and father, "I am going to make a lady out of Margaret." When she displayed talent on the piano, he did not hesitate to find one for her. In later years Ray's friendships would include one of the greatest vaudeville stars, singer Al Jolson. When the team was in New York Ray made a point of attending Jolson's shows and visiting with him afterwards. At times he received advance copies of the performer's records and sheet music, which he gave to Margaret to learn on the piano. When he returned to Herrin the Chapman home was filled with the latest Jolson standards, sung by Ray and accompanied by his younger sister.

At the Elks Club, where Ray spent much of his time, he and his fellow members came up with the idea of hosting a minstrel show for the local folks. Like Jolson, they put on blackface, startling Margaret, who was asked to sing before the main attraction. As appalling as it looks to us now, amateur minstrel shows in the early years of the twentieth century were still a popular draw, at least in the rural areas. The boys of the Elks Club would have seen no issue with what they did.

In January Ray received a phone call from Henry Edwards. As he did each winter, the sports editor wanted to get the latest scoop on Ray and key members of the ball club. In spite of all his travels, Ray had little to say. "There ain't any news here. So just write anything you want about me, and I will stand for it." Not much of a story, but the 1915 season would be a turbulent one for the shortstop and his ball club.

TO TRADE OR NOT TO TRADE

For the 1915 spring training, the Cleveland squad traveled long distance to San Antonio, Texas. Practicing in the hot, humid climate was hoped to be an antidote for the team's atrocious showing of the previous season. The players took to it, running through their drills with energy and purpose. While playing an exhibition in Waco, they rode out a major dust storm, winning the ballgame from the locals, 8–4. Home runs by Ray and Joe Jackson led the way.

At this spring training and many of the previous ones, the players had idle time in the evenings. In days past they had conducted "fanning bees," where the players gathered in the hotel lobby or on the front porch to talk baseball with anybody who dropped by. By 1915 fanning bees had morphed into the telling of tall tales. Yarns like these originated in the American frontier and continued post–Civil War through the Old West. Tales were told of real people such as Johnny Appleseed and Casey Jones, and of fictitious ones like Paul Bunyan and Pecos Bill. Cleveland had three players skilled in the art: Ray, Jack Graney, and pitcher Willie Mitchell. The three would gather after dinner to try and outdo each other with the greatest fib. One of Ray's favorites was the account of how he got his start in professional baseball.

While a teenager in Herrin, Ray needed to travel out of town. Having no money, he decided to stop by the railyard and "borrow a ride" on one of the freight trains. He found an open car loaded with sewer pipes, jumped inside, and made himself comfortable. About thirty miles later he spotted a ballpark with a game in progress. The train swung near the outfield fences just as the batter launched a drive to deep center field, heading out of the park. At the exact right moment Ray grabbed hold of the rail door with his right hand, leaned forward with his left arm out, and made a circus catch. He sat down, admiring his skill, only to notice several autos in hot pursuit of the train.

After another ten miles the engine slowed and the train came to a halt. Ray spied a police officer and three other men running toward him. The man in blue cited him for riding without a ticket in addition to stealing a baseball. "I plead guilty," Ray told the officer. "But it's my first offense. I never stole anything before except bases." One of the men then stepped forward with a document of several pages. He advised Ray that if he signed it the charges would be dropped. The document was a player's contract for the Toledo Mud Hens, giving him a salary of $400 a month. He quickly signed, beginning his professional baseball career. A great story, but likely the only truth was the "borrowed ride" on the train out of Herrin. Toledo was his third minor league club after Springfield and Davenport. The one-handed catch? A tall tale.

Another yarn concerned teammate Joe Jackson. Apparently Joe paid little regard to curfew hours, often arriving at the team hotels in the wee hours. Manager Birmingham advised him that he would be personally checking his room at 11:00 each evening. For several nights in a row Birmingham found Jackson's bed empty. The next night he checked again, again found Jackson not there, and headed back for the door. Jackson, in a childlike manner, sprang out from under the bed yelling, "Joe, I have been here every night!" The story got a lot of laughs but some bemused looks as well.

A tale that many claimed to be true concerned Ray and the flame-throwing pitcher Walter Johnson. Washington and

Cleveland were playing a late-season game that continued until darkness began to envelop the playing field. Ray came to bat, and two blazing fastballs he could barely see whizzed by him for strikes. Ray shook his head, stepped out of the batter's box, and walked toward the dugout. The home plate umpire, Billy Evans, yelled at him that he had another strike coming. Ray turned around and replied solemnly, "I don't want it!" Other versions of the story claimed Johnson's first pitch grazed the tip of Ray's cap, greatly alarming him, while the second pitch nearly scraped his jersey. The story would be told over the next fifty years in slightly different versions.

The exhibition season wound down with an April 4 game against the Pittsburgh Pirates. In the seventh inning Ray was called out on strikes by umpire Pender. Furious with the decision, he turned toward the umpire and with his bat against his chest shoved him backwards. They bickered for several minutes until Ray gave up and slowly walked to the Indians dugout. The 6,000 Pittsburgh fans stood up, showering the hapless umpire with obscenities. Why he did not toss Ray from the game is unclear.

In the ninth inning, with the game tied and a Cleveland runner on first, Ray tapped a slow roller back to the mound. The Pirates pitcher looked to second, then changed his mind and threw to first. Just as first baseman and former teammate Doc Johnston reached for the ball, Ray plowed into him, knocking the ball loose and sending it rolling down the right field line. As the go-ahead run came home, Honus Wagner and several of the Pirates came out of the dugout shouting furiously for an interference call. The next day the Pirates sportswriters called what Ray did a flat-out dirty play. What was he thinking in running down a vulnerable first baseman, someone he knew well from their days as rookies with the Naps? The game meant nothing, but maybe a supercompetitive player like Ray had to win, even if it meant possibly injuring someone. Luckily, Johnston survived the collision without any harm.

If this were the exhibition season, what would happen when the games counted? Ray's conduct was completely out of character, better suited for a hothead than the man who had addressed the Hawaii YMCA just four months prior. With the regular schedule only a week away, he needed to get his emotions firmly under control while concentrating on helping his team win the right way.

A short time later, Ray, perhaps trying to explain his behavior, told reporters, "We are just a bunch of boys who like to play baseball. Liking the game, we also like to win. We are going to make our own breaks. We are going to show the public the Indians do not know how to quit."

After a somewhat productive training camp, the Indians took a small amount of optimism into the start of the 1915 regular season. Larry Lajoie had been released after his long tenure with the ball club, forcing Charles Somers to drop the "Naps" nickname and find a new moniker for the team. There are several versions of how "Indians" became the choice, but the fans accepted it, as did the Cleveland sportswriters, who often fondly referred to the club as "the Tribe." The team name "Indians" would last for over a hundred years until the recent change to "Guardians." A new name meant a new era for the players, but whether they could turn things around and become competitive remained to be seen.

The always sanguine Ray Chapman, now hitting second in the batting order, believed this 1915 edition of the squad just might surprise people. He explained to reporters, "If there ever was a dark horse in the pennant race it is Cleveland this season. I never saw a more confident bunch in my life." Being optimistic is fine, but a lineup with unremarkable players such as Jay Kirke at first base, Walter Barbare at third, and Nemo Leibold in the outfield did not impress the oddsmakers. Joe Jackson might have a tremendous season, yet his presence did not translate to another twenty or thirty wins. Willie Mitchell and Guy Morton could pitch, but there was little else remaining of the staff.

Near the conclusion of spring training, the Indians were in Columbus for a final tune-up against the Senators. Catching for the American Association club was Bob Coleman, a one-time Davenport Prodigal from Ray's time in Iowa. Before the game Coleman threw down the gauntlet, advising his one-time teammate not to steal or he would be thrown out. In the course of the game Ray made certain to reach first base. On the first pitch he stole second, then on the next pitch stole third. Coleman, regarded as a good defensive catcher with an accurate arm, had nothing more to say.

On April 14, the campaign began with a road game in Detroit. An excellent crowd of 20,000 people was on hand along with four different brass bands to entertain. The Indians broke open a close game with three runs in the seventh inning to capture the opener, 5–1. Ray's two-run single highlighted the rally while Jackson knocked in the other tally.

The home opener took place April 22 against those same Tigers. Only 9,275 fans showed up at League Park as a steady rain kept most of the paying customers at home. In the top of the first inning pitcher Willie Mitchell set the tone by plunking Ty Cobb on the arm. Ray hit an infield grounder and proceeded to collide with Detroit's first baseman Marty Kavanagh. The ball came loose, but this time the umpire called him out for interference. If that was not enough, he later spiked Kavanagh in the heel. As did the Pirates earlier in the month, the Tiger players called out the Indians for dirty play. The new tactics, which the *Plain Dealer* called "scrappy," did not help the outcome of the game, as Detroit won 5–3. Ray had a two-run single in the sixth inning, his only hit of the game.

In town with the Tigers was Bobby Veach, now a rising star with the Tigers. He and Ray made a bet about who would have the higher batting average at season's end. The winner received a new hat. Detroit won three of four in the series, with Veach totaling eight hits, giving him a substantial early lead in the race for the chapeau.

At the end of the month Cleveland had a record of seven wins against nine losses. Fans stayed away from League Park, adding to the financial woes of owner Charles Somers. He was thought to have unlimited cash and assets, so it came as a major shock that he was mired in debt and would likely be forced to sell the ball club to become solvent. Several American League owners, Charles Comiskey included, let it be known that they would put up big money to buy Ray's contract along with Joe Jackson's.

Rumors floated of an offer of $15,000 plus three players to bring the shortstop to Chicago, where he would be moved to third base. Later the money attached was said to be $20,000, with names mentioned like pitcher Reb Russell and unheralded outfielder Tommy Quinlan. Somers had some grim decisions to make regarding his future in baseball. Should he sell Ray and Joe Jackson for about $40,00 to $45,000 to try to stay afloat for the season, or let the club go in hopes of settling his debts? The fans, what was left of them, wanted the ballplayers to stay, while they heartily agreed Somers should leave the game. They had seen a last-place team in 1914 and were faced with the prospect of another, unless Connie Mack's club beat the Indians in the race to the bottom. They would not support a losing team, eventually forcing Somers to show his hand.

An anxious Ray tried to concentrate on playing winning baseball. He was fond of Cleveland along with a particular twenty-one-year-old belle named Kathleen Marie Daly. Since he was now a major leaguer, his earlier views on the dangers of women were no longer an issue. Kathleen's father, Martin, who held a season pass to the home games, was the longtime president of East Ohio Gas Company, one of the largest utility companies in the United States. In addition to running a huge business concern, Martin was a trusted lieutenant of John D. Rockefeller, who owned the parent company of East Ohio Gas Company, Standard Oil.

On many different occasions, Kathleen, or "Katy," went to League Park with her first cousin Jane McMahon to watch the ballplayers cavort around the field. Usually they were chauffeured to the park, exiting the auto near the turnstiles while heads turned as they walked to their seats. Katy was tall and attractive, wearing only the latest of expensive fashion. Her red hair was shaped smartly in the "bob" style, cut just below the ears with bangs over her forehead. She had long, skinny legs, a family trait. To say she could make an entrance was an understatement.

Intrigued by Ray, Katy found mutual friends among her large circle of acquaintances to introduce her. They were a good match in that both had outgoing personalities, preferring to see the bright lights of the city rather than stay home and chat. And both were handsome people (even with Ray's hairline gradually thinning). Though they came from vastly different backgrounds, the two became an item.

Katy was raised from an early age to be a leading member of the women's aristocracy, sent to private schools and learning all the proper manners and graces of a young socialite. Her daily life revolved around attending luncheons while helping to organize charity events for the needy. A family member would later describe her as a "drama queen," somebody who needed a great deal of attention. That was possibly true, but women such as Katy had little choice but to stand out among her peers as her position in life dictated. In contrast, Ray came from a small town where most men were farmers and coal miners barely scraping out a living. Drama and attention were not called for there, making him more practical about how he conducted himself.

Katy lived in an affluent home in ritzy East Cleveland, on the eastern edge of Millionaire's Row. The family had a full-time cook, chauffeur, and other help to keep the large household running. Ray, in contrast, rented space in a rooming house within walking distance of League Park. His yearly salary with Cleveland was nickels and dimes compared to what Martin Daly earned in a month as president of East Ohio Gas.

One significant obstacle the couple had to deal with was religion. The Dalys were devout Catholics, active in the church as members of St. Philomena (across the street) in East Cleveland. Katy had attended a convent school then a private Catholic high school in Toledo, even remaining there to finish her education when the family moved to Cleveland. The few school records that exist show Katy as a dynamic singer and actress in the all-girl productions. As for Ray, he was Protestant, the same kid who ditched Sunday school to play baseball with his neighborhood friends. Ray would need to utilize all his charm and self-confidence to assure Katy's parents he could be a suitable man for her in all respects.

With a great deal weighing on his mind, Ray managed to produce some exciting moments on the baseball diamond. On May 22 the Indians were home to play Washington. With the Senators leading 6–5 in the bottom of the seventh inning, Ray tripled, then came racing home on an error to attempt to tie the game. Catcher Eddie Ainsmith had the ball in his grasp and was blocking the plate with all of his body. Ray slid hard, knocking the catcher off his feet and jarring the ball loose. Ainsmith tried to hold Ray down while the ball was recovered, but the shortstop pushed him off and scrambled to touch the plate safely.

Ainsmith followed Ray to the Cleveland dugout, challenging him to fight. The two squared off and punches were thrown before umpire Bill Dinneen got between them. The few fans in the grandstand roared their approval of the fisticuffs, happy to see some kind of life from their ball club. The Indians won the game in the twelfth inning, 7–6, on a Jack Graney single. In addition to the triple, Ray added a two-run single in the third inning, going 3 for 5 on the afternoon.

During the month of June, the team fell off the radar, dropping twenty of twenty-five games. Even with the lowest payroll in the American League, Somers's bankers would not allow him to put any more money into the team. The club held a firm position in sixth place, threatening to move even lower. Attendance was down to less than 3,000 per game, swelling the rumors of Ray being sent to Chicago or now Washington. Somers denied Ray was going anywhere, but the newspapers were packed with stories of four-player deals plus a large amount of currency to pry him loose.

The fans howled at the thought of Ray leaving Cleveland and returning in a different team's uniform. He was surely miserable, seeing his name in the daily papers as a hot candidate to be traded away along with Joe Jackson. Coupled with a budding romance with a Clevelander, the last thing he wanted to do was leave his adopted city.

June dragged into July with the trade rumors still boiling while the Cleveland ball club utterly fell apart. On July 13 at League Park the Indians faced the Boston Red Sox and their young pitching phenom, Babe Ruth. A costly error by Ray led to Boston's first two runs. In the bottom of the third with two men aboard and two out, the determined shortstop cracked a line drive far over center fielder Tris Speaker's head. Of all major league outfielders, Speaker was unsurpassed at turning his back and chasing down drives destined to be doubles or triples. On this occasion he could not get there; the ball rolled all the way to the scoreboard. Ray left the batter's box knowing he had a chance to circle the bases. He did not disappoint, crossing home plate without a slide.

The inside-the-park home run put Cleveland ahead 3–2, but Ruth slammed the door, not allowing any more runs while the Red Sox plated five more for an easy victory. The Indians went on to lose the series, 3–2, to further add to Charles Somers's woes. It became painfully obvious he could not count on attendance at the ballpark to help him out of a deep financial sinkhole.

The end of the month brought new lows for Ray and his teammates. At home against the Athletics on July 30, Ray strayed too far off first base and got caught in a rundown in front of second. A's shortstop Bill Kopf had an easy tag, but instead of facing the inevitable putout, Ray, with his take-no-prisoners mindset, lowered his shoulder and crashed into Kopf. Both players scrambled to their feet, with the A's shortstop throwing haymakers. Several players had to pull them apart. Another ugly incident in a dreadful season. Ray surely wanted to win, but this on-the-field behavior bordered on terrorizing the opposition. He needed to curtail his emotions, in all probability brought on by losing games and the nonstop trade talk.

More trade rumors followed, this time sending Ray to the Washington Senators for pitcher Joe Boehling, outfielder Danny Moeller, and infielders George McBride and Ray Morgan. A lot of bodies but not nearly enough talent in the proposed deal. A few days later Chicago entered the picture again, on this occasion a cash offer plus two players. Charles Somers still insisted, however, that his shortstop would remain in Cleveland.

On August 20 Somers sent Joe Jackson to the White Sox for a reported $31,000 and two players, outfielder Bobby "Braggo" Roth and pitcher Ed Klepfer. Somers told the press he needed the money and further stated, "Now I can positively say that Chapman will remain. There is not a club in the league but would pay big money for Chapman, but he is going to stay." He then visited the Cleveland locker room to reassure a worried Ray about his future.

The money from the Jackson trade ensured Somers would meet his payroll obligations through September, but more cash needed to be generated. Reports quickly surfaced that Ray was still on the market, with offers in the $25,000 range plus a few throw-in players. In late August, Tillinghast Huston, the co-owner of the Yankees, paid Somers a personal visit to orchestrate a deal that would send Ray to New York. Somers refused, reportedly saying, "Captain [Huston] I regard Chapman as worth more to me than you would be willing to pay." One can only guess the numbers thrown around. Thus ended the talks until at least after the season finished. The Indians dropped their last two games in October to finish with a miserable record of 57–95, good for a lowly seventh-place finish. They escaped the cellar only due to the ineptness of Connie Mack's Athletics, in last place with 43 wins and 109 losses.

Despite the nonstop distractions, Ray had his finest season to date, playing in all 152 games and batting .270, the third-highest total among major league shortstops. He scored 101 runs, fifth in the A.L., his 17 triples were third, and his 36 stolen bases ranked him seventh. His fielding numbers were improved, but his 50 errors were the third-highest total in the league. His .944 fielding percentage left him in the middle of the A.L. shortstops, but he had the top number of putouts, reflecting his ability to reach baseballs better than any other infielder. Though the year had been a trying one for all connected with Cleveland baseball, Ray managed to put together a good year, at times brilliant.

With the schedule concluded, Ray headed northwest to Crestline, Ohio, for a tournament in which four cities were represented. With several teammates joining him on the Crestline squad, Ray had four hits and four steals to help the host city win the tournament. Each of the Crestline players picked up some extra money. The players skirted the barnstorming rules by making a one-off appearance rather than staying together and traveling anywhere else. Ray did return to Cleveland to briefly join former Nap Bill Bradley and his "Boo Gang." With several of the Delahanty brothers along with other local ballplayers, Bradley had been scheduling postseason games around the Cleveland area for many years. Ray did his part then returned home to Herrin, set for another round of baseball.

The Herrin ball club had arranged a best-of-five series against the city of Marion for the southern Illinois championship. As player-manager for the home team, Ray led them to three victories in four games, complete with all the local bragging rights. In mid-November the folks in Herrin gave Ray a banquet at the popular Jefferson Café. A large crowd turned out to present him with a gold watch chain and a knife adorned with handsome diamond studs.

The *Herrin News* asked Ray about his plans for the winter. After his globetrotting the previous year, he told the paper, "I'm going to remain here all winter. When a fellow puts in about six or seven months with the leagues, he feels like taking off for a while and resting." He added that he would be making a quiet visit to Owensboro a few months later, then it was off to another spring training for the Indians.

At some stage in the off-season, probably around Christmastime, he made a visit to Cleveland to catch up with friends, his teammates, and his special girl, Katy. Having had a few months to think about it, he decided to ask the love of his life to marry him. He knew it would be complicated, trying to reassure his prospective father-in-law he was capable of giving Katy the lifestyle she had known since birth. How would he do this on a ballplayer's salary? Where would they live? Certainly not in Herrin or Owensboro. The choice had to be Cleveland, where all the finer things in life were easily available. Ray possessed a tremendous amount of charisma, but he needed more than that to make his future wife and in-laws accept him unconditionally. This undertaking would be more difficult than chasing a "Texas Leaguer" down the left field line.

The announcement appeared in print in the late winter of 1916, in the *Owensboro Messenger*, Ray's personal paper. The story read, "The Sporting News of this week announces that Ray Chapman, star shortstop of the Cleveland Club will be married to the daughter of a Cleveland gas magnate at an early date." The story was picked up nationally throughout the month and into early April. No other details were given, but the gas magnate would ultimately play a large role in orchestrating the engaged couple's years ahead.

Chapman home, ca. 2010. *Courtesy of the Chapman family.*

Cleveland Naps team photo, 1913. Ray stands in the top row, second from left. Lajoie is pictured third row, third from left, Joe Jackson second row, second from left. *Author's collection.*

Ray and several Nap teammates ca. 1913, presumably on a hunting and fishing trip. Ray is on the far right, next to Jack Graney and Larry, the dog. *Ohio University Libraries.*

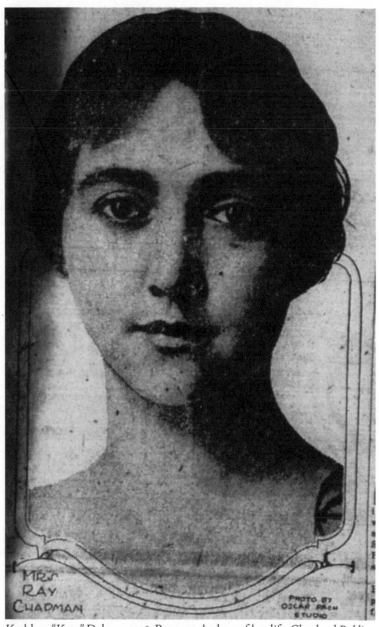

Kathleen "Katy" Daly, ca. 1916. Ray was the love of her life. *Cleveland Public Library Center for Local and Global History.*

Cigar advertisement, 1917, featuring Ray and Jack Graney. The boys received free cigars for hitting home runs. *Cleveland Public Library, Center for Local and Global History.*

Cleveland Indians team photo 1916. Ray stands fifth from left. *Library of Congress.*

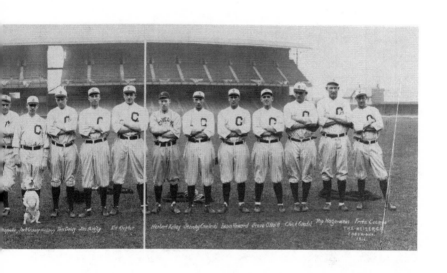

Reynolds, Jack Graney, Buddy Ryan, Tom Daley, Jim Baskette, Ed Klepfer, Herbert Kelley, Stanley Coveleski, Ivan Howard, Steve O'Neill, Chick Gandil, Nip Hagerman, Fritz Coombe

THE HEISER CO.
CLEVELAND
1916

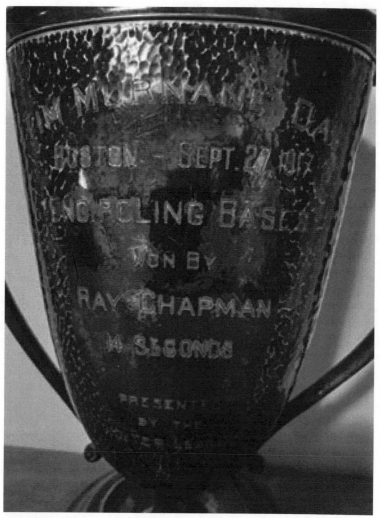

Ray Chapman trophy, 1917. Ray took part in pregame events at the Tim Murnane benefit game in Boston and posted the fastest time in circling the bases, fourteen seconds flat. *Courtesy of the Chapman family.*

Bill Wamby, 1918. He and Ray were one of the better double play combinations in the American League. *Cleveland Public Library / Photo Collection.*

Joe Wood, 1918. The former Red Sox pitcher-turned-outfielder was a close friend and pallbearer at Ray's funeral. *Cleveland Public Library / Photo Collection.*

Ray Chapman, 1918. With the season shortened for the war effort, Ray joined the Naval Reserve and sailed the Great Lakes. *Library of Congress.*

Martin Daly, ca. 1891. The president of the East Ohio Gas Company and Ray's father-in-law, Daly was exceedingly wealthy and built a home in 1920 for Ray and Katy as a wedding present. *Courtesy of the Daly-McMahon Family.*

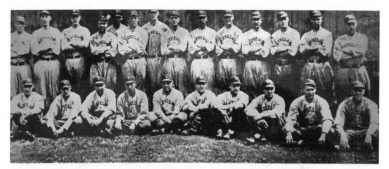

Cleveland Indians, 1920. One of the last photos taken of Ray. He is in the first row, fourth from right. *Courtesy of the Chapman family.*

The hearse carrying Ray to St. John's Cathedral, August 20, 1920. Due to the huge number of mourners, there was little room to bring the casket up the cathedral steps. Steve O'Neill and Joe Wood were among the pallbearers. *Author's collection.*

Ray's grave at Lakeview Cemetery, 1959. The large plot sits on a slight hill just off the road. *Cleveland Public Library / Photo Collection.*

A NEW FAMILY

Ray's future father-in-law, Martin Daly, was born in the early 1860s in Kingston, Ontario, Canada, the son of Irish Catholic immigrants. At an early age he moved with his family south of the border to upstate New York. There his father had a small farm, where the young son put his time in tending to the fields. Martin was a child of the Gilded Age, a period after the American Civil War when opportunities were plentiful for young men, regardless of their standing, to make their fortune. Success was measured by the money in your pockets. Railroads, oil, natural gas, and manufacturing plants were just a few of the industries rapidly expanding throughout the country. A man with intelligence, a capacity to learn, and aggressiveness might find himself a captain of industry and a millionaire. Martin did not have much formal education, but he possessed the intellect to advance beyond the static life on a farm.

As a teenager he left home, finding himself an entry position in the oil fields near Bradford, Pennsylvania. He worked at menial jobs, gradually advancing to office work and eventually to management. He had the aptitude for industrial organization, knowing how to build plants, unify personnel, and, most importantly, make a substantial profit for his bosses.

At the age of twenty-six he became supervisor of the Buffalo New York Natural Gas Company. With a large increase in pay, Martin courted and, in 1890, married Kathleen McMahon in nearby Ellicottville. The bride was the daughter of John Mc-Mahon, another Irish immigrant, who built houses in the area while operating two local sawmills. The marriage represented the union of a wealthy man with a woman of equal status. For a wedding gift the groom presented his bride with an elegant diamond broach set with rubies. The groomsmen received scarf pins adorned with diamonds and rubies.

A short time later Martin resigned from Buffalo Gas to take a superintendent position at the Northwestern Ohio Natural Gas Company. He settled in Toledo, eventually acquiring a home in the exclusive Old West End, where corporate executives and family-monied people lived. He became one of the directors and founders of Ohio Savings Bank while buying one of the local newspapers, the *Toledo News Bee*. It was in the upscale Glenwood Avenue home where their first child, Kathleen, the future Mrs. Ray Chapman, was born.

In the early 1900s Martin was asked to head up the newly created East Ohio Gas Company in Cleveland. With the blessing of John D. Rockefeller, Martin found a suitable plant with offices and started negotiations with Mayor Tom Johnson over gas franchise rights. With Cleveland a fast-growing city and houses converting to natural gas for heating, Daly built the company into a model for the rest of the country. Though he did it informally, workers who were out ill with serious illnesses or injuries received benefits from the company. If you were an Irish immigrant needing honest work, jobs digging pipelines or doing general maintenance could be had at East Ohio Gas.

When settled in Cleveland, Martin bought property on Euclid Avenue in East Cleveland, the place for the wealthiest folks in town. It would take time, but the Daly compound was built a block or two from the Rockefeller summer home. Here the five Daly children, three boys and two girls, would live until they went off to college or married.

In his spare time Martin liked to play cards, go fishing, and attend as many Naps/Indians games as he could. For several years he visited the ball club at their southern training sites, at times putting on a uniform and working out with the boys. He knew all the players by name, becoming acquainted with Ray Chapman in 1912. At no time then did he think about the popular shortstop becoming his son-in-law. Ballplayers could rub elbows with the well-to-do but were hardly encouraged to be on equal footing with them.

The intimate details of the engagement are not known, but Ray continued his life on the ballfield while Katy attended the opera and plays, often receiving mention in the society pages for her extravagant gowns and elegant dresses. At times she vacationed with her parents, traveling across the country for extended stays in the warm climate of Pasadena, California. She remained home for much of the baseball season to cheer on her fiancée at League Park. If necessary she drove her father's auto, being one of the few women in Cleveland with that privilege.

The 1916 season brought renewed hope to the Cleveland franchise. Eager and ready for spring training to begin, Ray forgot about the previous two years. In early February he wrote to manager Lee Fohl asking for permission to arrive in New Orleans early: "I feel that not only will I be getting in shape myself, but I will be able to help you in coaching the youngsters." He would report on February 20 with the pitchers and catchers.

Fohl agreed with the request and made Ray the unofficial coach of baserunning. Besides his 36 steals in 1915, no other Indian had pilfered more than 14. To say they needed help would not be an exaggeration. About Ray's transition to wise old veteran, the Cleveland manager said, "Chapman was a happy go-lucky sort of player for two years but during the last two months of the last season he became a student of the game." At twenty-five, Ray was maturing, realizing the necessity to learn the finer points of the game and set an example for the younger players.

Though he was serious in helping the younger players, Ray could not keep from playing a joke or two on them. During intrasquad games he would dash to cover second base, straddling the bag to catch the throw and tag out the runner. Seeing Ray, the newcomer would slide hard, only to see that the ball was somewhere else. The veteran would laugh and tell the victim he had to learn how to concentrate more.

Lee Fohl further elaborated on Ray's character and intensity in playing the game. "In fact, behind that cheery disposition Chapman is as earnest an athlete as ever wore a Cleveland uniform and not one of the tribe enthuses more over a victory or is more despondent because of a defeat than he." Most ballplayers try to remain on an even keel before and after games, attempting to avoid the highs and lows over a long season. But Ray let his emotions fly daily over each win and loss. Not the healthiest way to be, but apparently Ray could handle it, then be ready for the next ballgame.

In early March the players gathered for several practices along with the annual sore arms. By day two Ray could only field ground balls then roll them to second. The next day manager Fohl wisely decided to have only a brief practice, allowing the players an early change into their street clothes. Mardi Gras was winding down, and most of the players wanted to head downtown to mingle with the locals and thousands of tourists.

Ray's quest for maturity came into question when the Indians played a March 26 exhibition game. Newly acquired first baseman Chick Gandil was called out on a close play at second. It did not help that the umpire ruling on the play happened to be the same umpire Pender that Ray tangled with the previous spring training. Without warning Ray dashed onto the field, grabbed the startled umpire by the shoulders, and spun him around. An immediate ejection followed, but if Ray wanted to help the youngsters this was hardly the type of example to set.

Nonetheless, the sportswriters gravitated to Ray, knowing he was good for a story or quote they could use in their coverage of spring training. While some of the players were wary of reporters, Ray welcomed them to the locker room or back at the hotel. One of the writers asked him to name the six best pitchers in the American League. Surprisingly, Ray named Bert Gallia, a seventeen-game winner with Washington, as the tops in the league. He rated Gallia's teammate Walter Johnson second, despite his league-leading 27 wins, 203 strikeouts, and 7 shutouts. Prior to his 1915 season, Gallia had recorded just one major league win. Placing him first probably had to do with Ray facing him in 1912 while he was a Mud Hen and Gallia was with Kansas City. According to the Senators pitcher, Ray could not hit him when they were in the American Association.

Babe Ruth, with eighteen wins, did not make the cut, but George Dauss, the curveball artist with the Tigers, placed third, Ernie Shore of Boston fourth, Ray Caldwell of New York fifth, and Jim Scott, pitching for the White Sox, sixth. It was a good list but looked slightly out of order. Ray qualified his rankings by telling the writers, "I could name a lot of hard ones, for they are not hiring any easy ones. There may be pitchers ranking higher than some I named, but I judge them mainly by my own experience with them."

Before exiting camp, Ray asked a group of reporters if they had heard the story of Babe Ruth and one of his early starts in the American League. They reached for their pencils and notepads, knowing they had a good tale for the next day's papers. According to Ray, Ruth, at the beginning of his career, was pitching against Detroit on a late-season road trip. He had a three-run lead going into the bottom of the ninth inning. With two outs the Tigers got a baserunner. The next batter slammed one of Babe's offerings far over the right field fence. Ruth got the next hitter to end the game. On his return to Boston, a friend was waiting at the train station to greet the young pitcher. "Well, I see you beat the Tigers. Did they hit you very hard?" Babe answered, "The team didn't, but one guy slammed a ball almost out of sight. I didn't know anybody could hit 'em so far." The friend asked who the player was, and Babe said, "Oh I don't know. Some feller named Sam." He had no idea who Sam Crawford, one of the best and best-known hitters in baseball over the last decade, was. A great early Babe Ruth story, adding to Ray's growing list of tall tales.

The 1916 season brought renewed hope with major changes to the Cleveland club. In February James C. Dunn, a prominent contractor from Chicago, acquired the ball club from the bankers representing Charles Somers. He promised to shake things up, backing up his pledge by buying out Tris Speaker's contract from Boston. The game's greatest center fielder, at least defensively (Cobb could hit a wee bit better), was now coming to Cleveland for $50,000, a fabulous amount of money for any ballplayer. This giant step forward reinvigorated the fans even before opening day.

The four Cleveland newspapers got busy with the word that Speaker was on his way to join the Indians. They scurried around downtown, trying to find ballplayers to quote. Several reporters got a tip Ray was at a movie house. Looking for a good story, they burst into the theater and found their man seated in the audience. They walked outside with him and briefed him on the fantastic news. He responded, "Boys, we have three good outfielders but when I say that Speaker can cover almost twice as much ground as any one of them, you know I am about telling the truth."

His quote was completely legitimate. Tris Speaker was the finest outfielder in the game, blending speed and an uncanny ability to track down fly balls far over his head. His addition to the lineup negated the loss of Joe Jackson while making both corner outfielders better just by his presence. With Ray at shortstop, Bill Wamby at second, and Speaker in center field, Cleveland's defense up the middle became vastly improved.

On April 12 Cleveland opened its season at League Park, taking on the St. Louis Browns. For once there was no rain, but the fans were wearing overcoats due to the early spring chill. Ray committed two errors in the first inning, booting a ground ball, then dropping the throw at second from Jack Graney. A record crowd of 18,351 saw the disappointing 6–1 loss.

Despite the early miscues, Ray quickly improved his play, particularly when the club went on their first road trip of the season. Appearing in St. Louis in front of 23,000 Easter Sunday fans, Ray walked in the top half of the first inning. Speaker lined out to right fielder Jack Tobin, who nonchalantly lobbed the ball back to the infield. He failed to notice Ray tagging up at first then racing to second, beating the outfielder's lame toss. After George Sisler mishandled an infield grounder, he rounded third, then took off for home plate when pitcher Bill Fincher and Sisler exchanged some strong words, neglecting to watch the baserunner. Ray had two hits and three runs scored in a 14–2 pasting of the Browns.

When in St. Louis, Ray would often send for his sister Margaret to leave Herrin and join him for a few days in town. She would board the train, then ride a bus or a cab to Sportsman's Park. As she walked up to the ticket gate, Ray would always be there waiting, conversing with the ticket takers, who would let her in and show her to a seat.

After the game they would meet outside the park, where Ray would greet one or another of the newsboys there, saying, "Whose boy are you?" The young man would answer back, "I'm Chappie's boy!" and Ray would reach in his pocket and toss a few bills his way.

A few days later the White Sox came to town on Jim Dunn Day at League Park. Several bands, singers, and American League officials were on hand to honor the new owner of the Indians. The next day, with Cleveland ahead in the ninth, Chicago's Nemo Leibold led off with a single. With one out he attempted to steal. Catcher Steve O'Neill fired the ball to second, where Ray came over to cover the second base bag and apply the tag. Just as he arrived, his spikes caught in the ground, causing him to fall awkwardly forward. He lay on the ground for five minutes before getting to his feet and hobbling back to his position. The game ended with Cleveland winning 5–3.

In the locker room the team trainer examined the leg, thinking it only slightly twisted. Ray left the park for his rooming house, assuring reporters he would play the next afternoon. However, by early morning the knee had swelled up, resulting in a call to Dr. Castle. The examination revealed a more severe wrenching than previously thought. The doctor sent his patient to the hospital for at least two weeks or until the swelling disappeared. To ease the stay, game scores were fed to him on a daily basis.

Ray was sent on a train to Hot Springs, Virginia, to soak the knee in the warm waters. The treatment may have helped, but the shortstop would be sidelined until June 8, a period of six weeks. He did not start the game with Washington but entered as a pinch hitter for pitcher Jim Bagby. With a runner on first, he hit a sharp ground ball that the Senators turned into a double play. His knee was not yet ready for prime time, and he played sparingly until June 17 against the Yankees.

Two days later, while still facing New York, Ray got into a dust-up with first baseman Wally Pipp. In the second inning Pipp tried to steal second. His slide beat the throw, but Ray used his glove to push Pipp's leg off the base, resulting in an out call from the umpire. Pipp stood up and shoved Ray, who shoved right back. Several players got between the two before a slugfest could take place.

The incident added to the growing list of questionable behavior by the boy from Beaver Dam. Fights, shoving matches, lowering shoulders on people seemed to be part of the game plan. Some might call it dirty play, but in the context of the time period it came down to wanting to win more than anything else. If that meant bowling over a catcher to knock the ball loose or spiking somebody, he could live with the fallout without second-guessing himself. Being the competitor he was, he did whatever necessary to come out ahead.

Through July manager Fohl moved his infielders around to get the right combination. Ray found himself at third base for several games with Wamby at shortstop and Terry Turner at second. But gradually the pairing of Chapman at short with

Wamby at second began to fall into place. Over time they would become one of the best double play combinations in all of the American League.

At the end of July the Indians and Senators were tied at 1–1 in the top of the tenth inning. With a runner at second Walter Johnson laid down a sacrifice bunt. Ray, covering third, put the tag on the runner for what seemed an obvious out, but umpire Silk O'Loughlin gave the safe sign, prompting a near riot in the stands. In the tradition of the sport, pop bottles came flying at O'Loughlin from every angle. At game's end he would need a police escort to leave the park safely. The run eventually scored, allowing Washington to come away with the win.

A week later, on August 7, the Indians were home playing the Yankees. Ray had a tough time in the field, committing two errors, one on a dropped throw that led to a run. Several fans in the left field seats started to harass him with a selection of colorful words. New York won the game 3–2, and as Ray walked off the field one man in particular gave him an earful about his play. The stands at League Park were located close enough to the field, where the players could hear every taunt loud and clear. Frustrated by his own performance, the last thing he needed were insults from a boisterous fan. With several of the beat re-porters watching, Ray stopped just short of the grandstand and shouted at the jeering man, "If I were not a gentleman I would slap your face. I am not a rowdy however and do not believe in creating a scene." Several hundred people who were exiting the stands turned around and headed back to see what would hap-pen if Ray changed his mind. The fan, probably a touch fearful at being confronted by an angry ballplayer, shouted back, "If any apology is due you I am willing to make it. I want you to under-stand I am pulling for you and the entire Indians team."

Satisfied, Ray continued to the tunnel to the locker room and the fans dispersed, either happy or disappointed Ray had not jumped over the guardrail to pummel the loudmouth. The next day the crowd was supportive, cheering on the home team to a 9–4 win. Ray thrilled the onlookers when in the first inning he singled, then raced to third on a Speaker base hit to left field when the usual move was to play it safe and stop at second. In the sixth he hit a pop fly single to right field but never stopped running, stretching it into a double. Ray took his chances on the basepaths but possessed a knack for recognizing when he could take the extra base and get away with it.

In midmonth the Indians, with a respectable record of 62–51, went on an eastern road trip. They left New York for Boston on the overnight train, which would arrive in the early morning hours. The players asked one of the porters to rouse them about ten minutes before they reached the Back Bay station, an easy walk to the Lenox Hotel, where they were staying. The porter failed to remember, and when the train stopped only Terry Turner and manager Fohl were dressed and ready to leave. Seconds before departure the train blew its whistle and Ray, Speaker, and several other players dove off the steps and onto the platform. They had not shaved, combed their hair, or put on their shirt collars. Several of the startled commuters who were milling around the station looked around to see where the fire was. Seeing there was no blaze, the commuters went about their business while the ballplayers gathered themselves and marched to the hotel. The remaining members of the team slept peacefully on the train until the stop at South Station, where they found no cars or taxis waiting for them. They didn't make it to the Lenox until two hours later.

The season ended on a down note with the Indians losing nineteen of their last twenty-nine to finish in sixth place. Ray tried to shoulder the blame, telling the writers, "We infielders lost the pennant. If we infielders had only done our share at the bat and in the field." What he said was partially true, but the team had won twenty more games than the previous year, finishing only three games out of fourth place, a major improvement.

Ray's season fell far short of expectations, as he batted a mere .231 in 109 games. His knee problems played a role in his subpar stats, including his having only 21 stolen bases in 35 attempts. His great speed around the bases was not there, affecting his overall play for most of the year.

Jim Dunn made sure to come to the defense of his young shortstop, telling the *Plain Dealer,* "Chapman is a star player. He had a bad year this season, but he is one of those players who will not repeat. He is going to be a great help to us in finishing higher than we did this year." Dunn continued to earn points as the new Cleveland owner, demonstrating he had the players' best interests in mind.

Before going home to Herrin, Ray, Speaker, and Chick Gandil made their way up to the Canadian border to play several games around Ontario. Hopefully, the extra money was worth the trouble, because at the American League December meetings thirty-eight players, including the above trio, were fined for barnstorming. Among the wrongdoers were members of the World Champion Boston Red Sox, including Babe Ruth. The league showed it was serious, although it did rescind most of the fines before spring training.

At some point in those winter meetings, several teams made strong bids to acquire Ray and second baseman Bill Wamby. But once again Jim Dunn stepped up, telling the press, "If three such strong clubs as New York, Washington and Chicago made me offers for Ray Chapman or Bill Wambsganss [Wamby], I think those are two boys to hold on to."

Dunn was not averse to making deals, only those when he did not have the upper hand. Any trades for Ray and Wamby would have been pure foolishness unless names like Johnson or Collins were mentioned. Though to date his only major acquisition was obtaining Tris Speaker, over the next few years Dunn would make several trades that would change the course of Cleveland baseball history, putting Cleveland and Ray in position to challenge for the pennant.

7 SETTING NEW RECORDS

W hile Ray rested in Herrin, his fiancée was adding to her growing social portfolio. In late November Katy arrived in Toledo to christen a ship for the Standard Oil fleet. The auxiliary schooner *Daylite* was the sixth and last vessel in the company's "lite fleet." Katy served as the sponsor for the christening, which included an elaborate breakfast at the Toledo Shipbuilding Company. Her parents were in attendance and maybe had something to do with coordinating the event, but their daughter received full credit for the morning activities. As Ray grew his résumé in the baseball field, his wife-to-be advanced in society in Cleveland and parts of northwest Ohio. Absolutely a power couple in the making.

Katy had made her debut in 1910, attending the Cleveland Opera House to see a presentation of *Madame Butterfly*. Though many in the audience were opera buffs, others simply attended to be seen and if fortunate enough were mentioned in the next day's society pages. Mrs. Daly and her seventeen-year-old daughter got their name prominently mentioned in the right places.

By 1915 Katy was a regular in the uppermost part of Cleveland's social scene. In February she appeared in the play *The College Hero* at the Colonial Theatre. Along with twenty-three other young women, she played what the newspapers called a "realistic" basketball game, then tossed a number of silk balls into the crowd. It surely did not go unnoticed by Ray that his future wife could hold her own on the hardwood.

Several days later Katy hosted a charity ball at the Statler Hotel Ballroom to benefit a training home for young girls. The next day the *Plain Dealer* ran a story about the event with a flattering photo of the organizer. A few months later the papers covered another charity ball at the Statler, commenting on Katy's stylish blue velvet gown with lace trim. On New Year's Eve she hosted a dance party to benefit the Women's Club of Cleveland.

Katy's calendar was regularly filled with charity events to benefit a variety of social causes. At the Cotton Ball, held at Gray's Armory, the home for Cleveland's longtime volunteer military, Katy performed in a musical sketch, "Thirty Minutes in the Sunny South." The event raised money for the St. Ann's Maternity Ward Hospital. In a relatively short time, Katy was in demand all around the city, a must-have for the bluebloods at their well-to-do events.

In late December 1916 Ray visited Katy in Cleveland, along with friends in the city. He was enjoying the best things life had to offer: spending time with the Daly's, visiting family in Herrin and Owensboro, and carrying the status of a high-profile ballplayer. He had countless friends all over the Midwest and in the American League cities. There did not appear to be anything that could stop him in his rapid trajectory from small-town hero to national prominence.

While Ray enjoyed his downtime, events were taking place that would far overshadow the upcoming baseball season. World War I in Europe had been ongoing since 1914. With casualties in the hundreds of thousands, no end to the horrific conflict appeared imminent. Opinions in America varied regarding the potential military involvement of the country to aid allies like Great Britain and Canada. War fervor intensified when in early 1917 German U-boats began waging unrestricted warfare on any ships attempting to cross the Atlantic Ocean.

Cargo ships, passenger ships, and merchant ships were being attacked and sometimes sunk with no mercy.

In January of 1917 the infamous Zimmermann telegram became public knowledge. The German foreign secretary sent a top-secret document to Mexico and Japan asking them to join the fight with Germany against the United States. As a reward the countries would receive back property taken by the United States as far back in history as the 1840s! The plot bordered on ludicrous, but the majority of the American public was disturbed when the contents were revealed. As a result of this and other actions (such as the 1915 sinking of the *Lusitania*), serious discussions were taking place in Washington regarding a declaration of war against Germany.

As far as baseball was concerned, military drills would be conducted at training camps to show the willingness of the major leagues to be in lockstep with the general public. Most players would be marching with baseball bats, but rifles were coming. The possibility of a draft loomed in the months ahead, but for now the ballplayers reporting to spring training camps only needed to be concerned about getting in shape.

Ray left home for spring training on March 1. The first part of the New Orleans camp was easygoing, allowing him to play several rounds of golf with a new teammate, former Boston pitcher Joe Wood, and two local physicians. Tris Speaker did not arrive until March 17, meeting Ray and Wood at the ballpark for an early private workout. Even though Speaker had been with Cleveland for a relatively short time, he and Chapman had become the closest of friends. The outfielder shared an apartment with his former teammate Wood, but he gravitated toward Ray, often playing cards with him on the long, monotonous train trips.

At one point Ray introduced his new pal to Katy's cousin Jane McMahon. For a time they were quite a foursome, going about the town while others gazed at them with envy. Tris became enamored with Jane, buying her an expensive necklace as a show of his feelings. The romance carried on for a time before it fizzled out, leaving Ray and Katy to find other suitable couples to spend time with.

Spring training in New Orleans went by without almost any incidents. On March 31 the Indians played one of their last games in the "Big Easy." With the Indians leading by a lopsided margin in the top of the eighth, the Pelicans manager pulled out a bewildered middle-aged farmer from the stands and walked him to the pitcher's mound. Since the Pelicans had no chance to win, the manager thought he might get a big laugh from everybody at the park by having the man try to throw baseballs past the Cleveland batters.

The move was reminiscent of what Giants manager John McGraw did with Charles "Victory" Faust. In 1911 John McGraw was introduced to Faust, who claimed a fortune teller had told him he would pitch New York to the pennant. Being superstitious to a fault, McGraw let Faust stay with the team even though he had no talent for pitching or playing ball in general, and despite his showing obvious symptoms of mental illness.

With Faust on the bench, pitching batting practice, or in the bullpen warming up, the Giants went on a tear. He even pitched an inning or two during the regular season, much to the fans' laughter and delight. Once the Giants clinched the pennant, McGraw gave in to the clamoring from sportswriters and fans, sending Faust in to pitch the ninth inning against Boston. Though he had nothing on the ball, he survived, then pitched again, this time facing Brooklyn for an inning. The teams made certain to let Faust bat, and ran him around the bases, having him slide at each one while the grandstand howled with laughter. Unfortunately, Faust did not have the capacity to understand that the joke was on him. A colorful version of this story was delivered by old New York outfielder Fred Snodgrass in the landmark book *The Glory of Their Times,* by Lawrence Ritter.

In this instance the New Orleans gentleman had no choice but to go through the mockery. The first two Cleveland hitters to face Mr. Williams, or "Mathewson" (as announced by umpire Moriarty), were Jim Bagby and Jack Graney, who clowned around while batting. Ray came to the plate dressed in a catcher's mask and chest protector. He tried to bat one of the slow balls with his mask, but the ball hit him on top of the head, fortunately with no damage. He went on to strike out. Speaker also came to bat with a chest protector and also struck out, swinging wildly three times to end the inning.

In the ninth all three Cleveland hitters bunted and walked toward first, letting "Mathewson" tag them out even though he fell down several times in the process. They made sure to have the old person bat and let him hit a slow roller for a base hit. They got him to slide at second base, much to the hilarity of all in the park. To end the burlesque, Ray grabbed the man near second, holding him while Jack Graney ran in from left field and tagged him out.

The ballplayers were not, as it may have seemed, being intentionally cruel. In their defense, their lack of thoughtfulness toward those who might be lacking skills or common sense was not generally considered offensive in the early twentieth century. They had no concern about any blowback. The newspaper reporter who wrote the account and the editor who reviewed it saw it only as comical.

On April 2 President Woodrow Wilson went before Congress to ask for a declaration of war. It took two days for the House of Representatives to approve, then two additional days for the Senate to follow suit, and as of April 6, 1917, the United States was officially at war with Germany. A large army needed to be raised as soon as possible to join the fight in Europe. Whether major league ballplayers needed to be concerned had not yet been determined.

The ball club broke camp at New Orleans and headed north, stopping in selected cities for further exhibitions. On a windy and cold April 10 they arrived in Toledo to play against Ray's former club. About 1,200 fans were scattered around the park, shivering in their overcoats. In the top of the second inning the bases were loaded when Ray launched a ball far over the outfielders to the base of the scoreboard. He circled the bases for a grand slam home run, his second of four hits in the 13–0 rout. Without question he was ready to play ball.

The regular season opened on April 11 at Detroit. With the declaration of war, the game took on added significance as a patriotic event. An overflow crowd watched both teams go through somewhat serious military drills and a flag raising, while for the first time the local bands played "The Star-Spangled Banner" at Navin Field. The Indians won the game 6–4.

Ray, eager to make up for his poor showing in 1916, came out of the gate with bat blazing. By May 4 he had a batting average of .324, 22 hits, including 9 doubles, 14 runs scored, and 9 sacrifices. He had only 3 stolen bases, but that number would soon pick up. He was already silencing his critics from the past season. The *Plain Dealer* wrote, "One factor in the Indians getting into the first division is the return of Ray Chapman to the form he displayed in 1915 when he was known as the best shortstop in the league."

On May 14 Cleveland hosted the Red Sox at League Park. Although credited with only one at bat, Ray had an exceptional day. In the bottom of the first he sacrificed Jack Graney to second to help key a three-run inning. He drew a base on balls in the third frame, then stole second and third before scoring on a single by Bobby Roth. In the fourth inning he drove in a run with a sacrifice fly, and in the sixth he singled. In the home half of the eighth he walked for the second time, but only remained there a moment, stealing second then third again for a total of four steals in the game. Cleveland won 7–6. With Ray and Speaker leading the way, the Indians were clearly an improved team.

The much-anticipated war draft became official on May 18 with the passing of the Selective Service Act. All males between the ages of twenty-one and thirty were required to register on

June 5 or face severe penalties. Large pieces of major league rosters thus had eligible men liable for service. How the government planned to use the huge pool of potential recruits would be sorted out later in the summer.

American League president Ban Johnson, after meeting with several army generals, believed few players would be drafted until October. He was confident that the teams taking part in drills would suffice at least for the current season. In an editorial the *Sporting News* thought direct assurances from the military were not appropriate, but a general assumption prevailed that the players were unofficially exempt. The paper asserted that the general public supported the idea of a complete baseball season.

On June 1 Boston and Babe Ruth were facing the Indians at League Park. The Red Sox pitching star already had 10 wins to his credit, while Guy Morton, on the mound for Cleveland, had a grand total of one victory. With one out in the fourth inning Ray singled, and after Speaker flied out he stole second. Bobby Roth swung at a third strike, but catcher Chet Thomas could not hang on to the ball, which rolled to the backstop. Roth raced to first then rounded the bag as if to try to take another base, while Ray edged down the third base line, looking for a chance to dash home. An alert Thomas saw him and fired a peg to third, trapping Ray between third and home. After several throws back and forth Ray appeared to be dead in his tracks, but as Thomas went to tag him he adeptly lowered his body then rushed past Thomas to elude the rundown and reach home safely.

Few players survive a rundown, but Ray miraculously dodged three different Red Sox to score an important run. Cleveland won the game 3–0, handing Ruth only his second defeat of the season. By now the newspapers were referring to Ray as a "daredevil on the bases," an accurate description.

After a brief homestand the Indians traveled to Washington for a three-game series. Greeting them in the capital was a Cleveland physician, Dr. Bob Drury, on his way to France to head up a field hospital for wounded soldiers. After some small talk he asked Ray to go with him to assist with the logistics. A daunting task for sure, and Ray politely declined. It is not clear if he would have been a civilian volunteer or needed to enlist, but like the vast majority of ballplayers he intended to wait to be called rather than step forward.

June 5 rolled around with half the clubs, including Cleveland, on the road and unable to stop at their local draft boards for registration. Special arrangements would have to be made on their behalf. At some later date Ray would find his way to Herrin and get himself registered for service. He would comment, "For my part I regret that I did not enlist last spring and try for a commission. If I am called in the draft I will not waste any time in laying aside the baseball uniform and getting into the khaki." His late entry into the registration process left him about halfway down the list of eligible men from Herrin.

A few weeks later the June 24 edition of the *Owensboro Messenger* carried a feature on their favorite ballplayer. The paper had been biding its time to run such a piece but believed the moment was now. The story began, "Ray Chapman is playing the best game of his career. He is the best shortstop in the league. This is no extravagant claim inspired by friendship or partisanship. It is the truth. The figures speak for themselves." The paper went on to post Ray's fielding statistics from May 20 through June 15, showing just two errors with thirty-five putouts and fifty-six assists. A highlight was a doubleheader against Washington, where he handled nineteen chances without a miscue. The newspaper was clearly bursting with pride about their adopted favorite son, and now the figures supported their claims.

Near the season's halfway point, Ray and his teammates began to play at a blistering pace. The core lineup of Steve O'Neill catching, Jim Bagby and Stan Coveleski pitching, Wamby at second, Ray at short, and Speaker in center field was receiving notice around the American League. Just as the folks in Owensboro knew, Ray was having his finest season as an Indian, doing all the right things on offense and defense. All season he was among the leaders in runs scored, steals, and sacrifices, and defensively in putouts and assists for shortstops. His batting average hovered around .300 for much of the campaign. His feats on the base-paths were extraordinary, manufacturing runs whenever needed.

On July 22 the Indians destroyed Philadelphia at home, putting up a football score in a 20–6 rout. With a runner aboard, Ray smacked his first home run of the season, going 3 for 6 for the day with three RBIs. His big afternoon did not go ignored, as on the next homestand in August Paramount Cigars, a Cleveland company, awarded him and Graney a box of fresh cigars each, apparently because Jack had recently homered as well. The two posed for a photo, smiling to the camera while clutching their gifts. The following day in the *Plain Dealer* a quarter-page ad appeared on the sports page with the ballplayers' images. The caption read in large letters, "Worth Trying For," then "Here are two Cleveland players who are happy." Evidently Ray and Jack agreed to be photographed and take part in the ad in return for the free cigars. A good trade for both parties.

By mid-August the Indians were a distant third, trailing the White Sox and second-place Boston by a large margin. On Sunday the twelfth they played Chicago at home in front of a crowd totaling over 20,000 fans, with hundreds swarming behind ropes in left center field. Those in attendance let out a roar as several companies of army engineers smartly paraded around the playing field. The game itself was a nail-biter. With the Sox leading 3–2 in the bottom of the ninth, Jack Graney tied the score with a double, bringing Ray to bat with a chance to bring home his roommate and win the ballgame. All eyes were on him when he scorched a rising line drive toward left field. Before the fans could jump out of their seats, shortstop Swede Risberg made an impossible leap, snaring the ball and sending the game to extra innings. Despite a double by Ray in the twelfth, his third hit of the game, Chicago won in thirteen innings, 4–3. The loss put the lid on any hopes of an eleventh-hour rally to overtake the Sox.

In September, while playing the Athletics on the road, Ray walked in the first inning, stole second, went to third on Speaker's fly out, then stole home for the first run of the game. In the eighth inning he swatted a double, stole third, and scored on Speaker's ground out to second. Cleveland won the game 5–4 with Ray's legs leading the way.

On the twenty-seventh, Ray, Speaker, and O'Neill participated in a benefit All-Star game in Boston for the late Tim Murnane, a former player and longtime sportswriter for the *Boston Globe*. Most of the teams had the day off. The American League stars, including Ty Cobb, Joe Jackson, Walter Johnson, and the three Indians, played the Red Sox, with all proceeds going to Murnane's wife and children.

To attract fans to the ballpark, a series of events was scheduled to take place before game time. One was a race around the bases to determine the fastest man in the American League. Ray took his turn in the batter's box, holding a bat in bunt position. At a signal he dropped the bat and raced around the bases, picking up speed as he went. He crossed the plate with a blazing time of fourteen seconds flat, the best time of any of the competitors. For his efforts, the events committee awarded him an engraved silver trophy, which his family still keeps. As another memento, Ray swiped the umpire's broom to go along with the handsome award. The dust on the broom was probably his.

The 17,000 fans in attendance got their money's worth watching Joe Jackson hurl a baseball 396 feet and Babe Ruth lift a fungo a whopping 402 feet. Popular cowboy comedian Will Rogers rode his horse around the field doing fancy tricks with his lariat. Moments later Speaker and Cobb appeared, galloping two horses the length of the grounds. The Red Sox defeated the All-Stars 2–0, with Ray getting a base hit for the stars. Afterwards the three Cleveland players hurried to catch a train to Washington for the next day's game.

Ray would finish the season with 52 stolen bases, third in the league behind Ty Cobb and Eddie Collins. For sixty-three years that number stood at the top of the Cleveland all-time records until broken by Miguel Dilone, a light-hitting outfielder with great speed. Ray's 67 sacrifices were best in the junior circuit, breaking the record of 60 by Bill Bradley of the Cleveland Naps back in 1908. Ray's 98 runs scored were third, while he batted a career-high .302. On the defensive side his putouts and assists were best in each category. *Baseball Magazine* would name him to their All-Star team, saying, "Among shortstops Chapman is the season's best. His record is one that fairly scintillates."

After the completion of the regular season and a third-place finish for the Indians, Ray found himself as busy as ever. In a postseason series against the Cincinnati Reds (sanctioned by the American League), the Indians lost the championship of Ohio, four games to two. Ray hit a dismal .174 in the series but managed to hold up his end on defense. After the series was completed, both teams honored a request to play one more game in Chillicothe, Ohio, to entertain the soldiers at Camp Sherman. On a makeshift field in front of 4,000 eager soldiers perched on a nearby hillside, Cleveland beat Cincinnati 3–1, and the players gave seven dozen baseballs to the military men plus an autographed ball to the camp commander.

Ray then joined Tris Speaker for a 1,500-mile ride to Speaker's hometown of Hubbard, Texas, for several weeks of relaxed hunting and fishing. Speaker had purchased a camper trailer in which he and Ray would stop for the night and sleep under the stars. Just two old country boys taking in the sights. The two buddies made a quick detour to Owensboro, where Tris was introduced to the Johnson side of the family. Then they were back on the road, where Jim Dunn managed to track them down, asking if they would stop in Montgomery, Alabama, to play an exhibition game for 10,000 troops stationed there. Though both were in real need of some time off, they unselfishly agreed. They arrived in early November, joining Steve O'Neill and Jim Bagby. The soldiers were thrilled when Ray got on base and trotted home ahead of Speaker's long home run. Then finally it was on to Texas for the much-delayed hunting and fishing to begin.

Ray returned home to Herrin to visit with the Chapmans. In early March of 1918 he received his classification from the Du Quoin, Illinois, district as A-1 for the draft. Of the 716 men registered in the area, Ray was officially number three hundred, meaning he had better than a 50 percent chance of being called for duty. He indicated that when summoned he would take his physical exam in Herrin then leave from there for boot camp. Already eight members of the Indians were classified 1-A, including Bill Wamby and reserve catcher Josh Billings. Many major league ballplayers were in the same boat as Ray, including Grover Cleveland Alexander, George Burns (American League), Harry Heilmann, and Red Faber.

Regardless of the war situation, players reported to New Orleans intent on at least starting the season. In late March Ray became quite ill with a stomach ailment, losing nine pounds in just a matter of days. He was put on a diet of toast and milk until he felt well enough to eat the amount of food an athlete in training requires. He recovered quickly, taking part in the exhibition games and the famous exploding golf ball incident, where Steve O'Neill teed up the loaded ball and took a mighty wallop, only to see it detonate into a thousand pieces. The players were loose and having fun, a good sign for the upcoming schedule.

With his health completely restored, Ray added to his standing as the premier tall-tale artist on the club. While relaxing at the De Soto Hotel in New Orleans, he recalled a story about pitcher Red Torkelson, a 1917 late-season addition to the Cleveland roster. In a game against Washington the new recruit cruised through the first three innings. In the fourth he loaded the bases, bringing outfielder Mike Menosky up. Torkelson threw two quick strikes, then turned toward Ray at shortstop and winked, as if to say, "This is easy." He wound up and delivered the pitch plateward, where Menosky swung, hammering the ball over the right field wall for a grand slam home run. That was the last wink from Torkelson, who soon returned to the minor leagues.

Another of Ray's tall tales involved roommate Jack Graney, the rival storyteller. The outfielder was getting dressed for a game at League Park when a small boy climbed the high brick wall and peered into the locker room. The boy said, "Oh Jack, hit one over the right field screen so I can get into the game, will you?" The Cleveland ticket office always granted free admission for any returned baseballs. Graney answered, "Kid, if you wait until I hit one over the screen, you will trip up on your whiskers!"

While still in camp, Ray described his greatest game played to the *Plain Dealer*. It was the contest in 1912 with the Toledo Mud Hens while Rube Waddell was pitching for Minnesota. Not only did he have five hits, but he stole home and scored four runs while handling nine chances without an error. Surely a tremendous performance, but there were many more to come over the next three seasons.

RAY JOINS THE NAVAL RESERVE

The Cleveland home opener with Detroit was scheduled for Monday, April 16, but heavy rains kept the players off the field for two full days. Another factor keeping the boys away from the diamond was the "grippe" spreading through both teams' rosters. One of the first to go down happened to be Ty Cobb, who was confined to his bed at the Hollenden Hotel in downtown Cleveland. Pitcher Willie Mitchell found himself admitted to a hospital nearby with symptoms of pneumonia, closely associated with the influenza.

Jack Graney, Ray's roommate, was the initial Cleveland player to become ill, unable to leave the boardinghouse neighboring League Park. Within days almost half the Indians roster would be sidelined. The newspapers simply reported the players out with the grippe, showing little worry about an illness that was about to ravage the United States and much of the world. The first wave of the pandemic, which many incorrectly called the "Spanish flu" (it did not originate there), landed at the Eastern Seaboard army bases in the United States and quickly spread state by state. This first wave carried a virus that became lethal for the older population more than those who were young and active. The ballplayers were fortunate in being fit enough to swiftly fight off the symptoms and return to full strength in a matter of three or four days. But given their constant exposure to the virus from riding the trains, crowding into cabs, and frequenting restaurants while on the road, it was a matter of chance that relatively few major league players were seriously affected by it.

Health officials were urging the population to wear masks, stay home, and limit large gatherings. Their sound advice had little effect on the major leagues, as fans jammed into parks, oblivious to the chances they were taking. It is unknown how many fans in 1918 went to the ballparks, became ill with the virus, and perished within a short time. In Cleveland, opening day had on hand 250 Naval Reservists along with 500 Elks from Detroit. Those figures alone were enough to spread the virus throughout the city.

The second wave began at the end of the season, picking up steam as the ballplayers were heading home, away from many of the highly contagious areas. The only fatalities of note with recent connections to the game were retired outfielder Matty McIntyre, who had spent most of his career with Detroit; Larry Chappell, a reserve outfielder who last played in 1917; and "Silk" O'Loughlin, the revered longtime American League umpire.

The opener took place on April 18. With a steady rain throughout the afternoon, 11,000 people watched Cleveland defeat Detroit, 6–2. Ray did nothing to distinguish himself, only scoring on a three-run triple by outfielder Bobby Roth in the bottom of the seventh inning. The Tigers were still missing Ty Cobb and Willie Mitchell, not yet recovered from the sickness. There were likely more than a few other ballplayers ill from the influenza, but the newspapers in the major league cities for the most part glossed over it.

Sunday, April 21, was "Liberty Loan Day" at League Park and several locations around Cleveland. Jim Dunn kicked things off by buying $2,000 in government bonds for himself and his wife. Ray dug deep into his pockets, buying $500 worth, setting a superb example for all the ballplayers to match or better. Twelve young ladies canvassed the stands for contributions, bringing in $7,000 more in pledges. Despite an 11–7 loss to the Browns, most who were at the park went home in a lighter mood.

LOVE AND LOSS

The series with St. Louis continued on Monday. Ray had a terrific afternoon. In the first inning he singled, stole second and third, then scored when Browns pitcher Dave Davenport hit Marty Kavanagh (now a Cleveland player) with the bases filled. Two innings later he walked, reached second on a ground ball, stole third, and scored on Roth's single. Another single and walk produced two more runs scored, giving him four runs in three official times at bat, which accounted for half of Cleveland's total in the 8–1 win.

With the crowds at League Park and a roommate carrying the virus, it was bound to happen. Ray reported to the sick bay on the evening of the twenty-fourth with symptoms including a fever plus aches and pains. He missed the April 25 game at Detroit, along with the rest of the Cleveland infield. Wamby and Terry Turner had fevers of 102 degrees, and Jim Bagby's reached 103.5. Studies showed that fever from the influenza ranged from 101 to 105 degrees. Another couple of degrees would likely have meant grave complications for the stricken players.

Despite having to start replacement players at all four infield positions, the Indians managed to win the game, 8–4. Ray benefited from a rainout on the twenty-sixth and by the next day had shaken off the symptoms enough to appear in the series finale. The game was deadlocked in the top of the twelfth inning when Ray leaned into one of pitcher Bill James's offerings and lined the ball into the seats for a tiebreaking home run. Detroit could not answer in the bottom of the inning, and Ray's hit was the difference in the 3–2 victory.

Maybe it was seeing the 250 sailors on hand on "Liberty Loan Sunday" at League Park, or maybe he had already been giving it serious thought, but on May 2 Ray sent a telegram to his uncle J. R. Johnson that he had enlisted in the Naval Reserve. He added that his report date had not been finalized and it might be possible to play ball up to September. Ray made a shrewd decision in becoming a reservist, knowing the chances of being called overseas were minimal. In all likelihood, he would not leave the Great Lakes area, staying worlds away from the fighting.

While the new recruit bided his time, a highly complimentary article appeared in a Pittsburgh newspaper, saying, "A .300 hitter with remarkable running ability, Chapman is a consistent athlete who probably means more to a winning ball club than a Cobb or Sisler because he is on the first line of defense and in the most difficult job on this important line of action." Though Cobb and Sisler were two of the elite hitters in the game, the reporter believed Ray had more value to his club in terms of overall play. Given that Pittsburgh was a National League city, Ray's impact on the field had clearly drawn a lot of attention outside Cleveland and the American League cities.

On Friday, July 19, the government issued the "Work or Fight Order," obliging all eligible males to find a job in the defense industry or be drafted into service without delay. The edict threw major league baseball on its ear, forcing an abrupt appeal to secretary of war Newton Baker and the War Department to allow the season to play out. Ray announced he would report for duty in the next several days if the season were to end but would wait until Monday before leaving the team. By Sunday he had his bags packed.

However, news came of a probable compromise that would grant a shortened schedule to the teams, possibly through September 1. Ray waited a few more days for a decision. The next Friday brought official news that the season would end on September 1, followed by a World Series. The ruling gave the ballplayers time to determine a course of action and the owners another two months plus of revenue. Given the circumstances, this was a generous concession from the government, which was under no obligation to do anything for the owners and players.

The season played out through August with Cleveland in second place, within striking distance of first-place Boston, but running out of time. After completing a series in Philadelphia, the Indians players had a day off on the twenty-ninth, then

LOVE AND LOSS

would travel to Detroit and Chicago to finish the schedule. With a free day in Cleveland, Ray played for the Naval Reserve team, nicknamed the "Jackies," against Standard Parts, a top-class AA amateur team. The sailors won the game 5–4, with Ray to be named player-manager as soon as he reported for duty. The Jackies were scheduled to play ballgames every weekend through September, and Ray was expected to organize the roster along with playing each Sunday.

Before leaving for Detroit, Ray collected a silver identification card case from the ball club in acknowledgment of his upcoming service in the navy. Speaker, Wamby, and Josh Billings received gold watches (Ray already owned one) for their impending entry into the armed forces. The players who chose to work in the defense plants got a thank you and a pat on the back.

On Sunday, September 1, the season ended in Chicago as the second-place Indians went out on a winning note, 8–5. Ray celebrated the final day with three base hits in four tries. He led the American League in runs scored with 84 and was third in steals with 35 and second in sacrifice hits, also with 35. His 84 walks, first in the league, showed more patience at the plate and a better command of the strike zone. On the defensive side he once again led the league in putouts, though his 50 errors came in as second-most among all American League fielders. He was not quite a finished product, but he continued to be regarded as the best shortstop in baseball.

A day or two later Ray entered the navy as an ordinary "gob," or plain sailor. He did not ask for any type of commission or special treatment, planning to serve as an ordinary second-class seaman. It did not take long for his commanding officers to see the potential in their new recruit. Within days Ray was enrolled in officer training school, located east of downtown Cleveland. He studied hard there and was in line for a transfer to the Pelham Bay, New York, Naval Training Station to earn his gold stripe. As an ensign or second lieutenant he would be qualified to command crews and petty officers while at sea.

While he was still stationed in Cleveland, his tour of duty would be on the *H. H. Rogers,* involving nighttime patrols up and down Lake Erie and the Detroit River, where he often served as a lookout. While Ray peered through his binoculars, his shipmates defended the citizens of northeast Ohio and southeastern Michigan from any unusual activities, including phantom attacks by German U-boats.

The probability of any warfare on or about the Great Lakes was just about zero, but the boys took their assignments in good form, doing their jobs respectfully. Serving on the lakeshore allowed Ray to see his fiancée on weekends, but any marriage plans were placed on hold until the conclusion of the war.

On Sunday, September 14, Naval Reservists were part of an exhibition at League Park that included boxing, track and field events, and bayonet drills from the 310th Army regiment. Ray won the 100-yard dash in an impressive 10.45 seconds. Later in the afternoon he played shortstop for the Reserves, getting two hits in a 4–0 win over Michigan's Camp Custer. Most of the money taken in went toward a fund for widows and orphans of those killed in battle. Though not in the fight on the North Atlantic, the local sailors were doing their part for the war effort.

At the end of the month the Canteen Club opened at Thirty-Fifth and Euclid, a place for soldiers and sailors to gather to dance with sociable young ladies and or chow down on some home-cooked food. The location was actually the Woman's Club, where Katy took part in various fundraisers for the war and other charitable causes. On Sundays she could meet Ray, if he wasn't playing ball, for an afternoon of pulling taffy and making popcorn balls. Canteens played a significant role during the war in helping the enlisted men unwind and temporarily forget their troubles.

Rumors floated that Ray would be joining the Reserves football team to play halfback in games against colleges and army and navy squads. The stories must have startled Jim Dunn as several days later the local gob announced he would stick to baseball. It was one thing to be wounded overseas on a battleship, but to break an arm or leg playing football would not be the wisest thing to do.

On the last Sunday in September and into October Ray confined himself to baseball with the Reserves and a group of Cleveland All-Stars. This club had an outstanding lineup featuring Lajoie at second base, Ray at short, Terry Turner at third, Josh Billings catching, and Jack Graney playing left field next to Dode Paskert, a National League outfielder and Cleveland resident. Life in the navy had its perks!

While Ray faithfully patrolled Lake Erie, the German army surrendered to the Allies on November 11, 1918, ending four years of bloody conflict. Though U.S. forces were active for just a year and a half of that time, the casualties were considerable. A total of 116,000 men died, while over 200,000 were wounded. Over half the deaths were from sickness and disease, with the vast majority of those credited to the ongoing pandemic. The influenza spread in another wave from base to base, home and abroad, killing many before they ever stepped on the battlefield or shipped out of the States. The lucky ones were those who stayed out of the fight, serving at home, where somewhat better sanitary conditions prevailed, although a number of the bases were overrun with the virus and saw subsequent deaths. The Naval Reserve facility in Cleveland had few if any cases, allowing Ray to avoid a second bout.

Now that the "war to end all wars" had come to a close, the soldiers and sailors eagerly waited for their discharges. Ray's plans to transfer to Pelham Bay were canceled. The war ending in November was fortunate for him, because the Bronx training station was full of desperately sick men. In the fall and winter months the base recorded over 2,000 cases of the virus and 145 deaths.

On December 2 Ray left Cleveland for the University of Pittsburgh for a football game between his fellow Reserves and the college eleven. Ray was not on the roster but talked his way into being one of the referees. He made his presence known with just under five minutes left in the first half. Pitt had an excellent drive going inside the Reserves' ten-yard line with ample time to score when Ray shouted that the half was over and motioned for the teams to leave the field. The other referees were startled but did nothing; halftime had been declared and a likely touchdown by the college saved.

Into the third quarter a highly partisan Ray tried to intimidate the other refs, arguing about any calls against his sailors. Though he had been a sailor for only a little over three months, Ray had learned all he needed to know about life at sea, including the ability to use curse words like no other branch of the service. Seafaring men spent long periods shipboard, mostly with no women or children about. They worked hard, drank their weight, and swore when they felt the urge. Ray made the phrase "swear like a sailor" his own, unloading all the foul language known to man at the other referees and shocking players and coaches alike, including Pitt's revered coach, Glenn "Pop" Warner.

The Pittsburgh newspapers had a field day trashing the so-called referee from the Reserves. One wrote, "One of the most disgusting exhibitions of unfairness was the action of Ray Chapman who in every way possible harassed the head linesman and attempted to stop him from calling Cleveland men offside." Others used such phrases as "Using language unfit to repeat" and "The most foul language ever heard on a ball field." The stories were reprinted all across the country, painting Ray as the worst kind of navy man. It is one thing to be ultracompetitive and break a rule or two, but Ray stepped well over the line in this instance.

A few days later second baseman and army lieutenant Bill Wamby arrived in Cleveland after his discharge. Sportswriters peppered him with questions. What would he do first: Visit family? Go out for a steak dinner? Wamby smiled. "I think I will go over to the Naval Reserve's headquarters tomorrow for I want to see Chapman and Billings salute me." Apparently a big laugh was the junior officer's top priority.

By January of 1919 Ray had received his discharge too. He called his time in the navy "one of the greatest experiences in my life." It was home to Herrin, then on to Owensboro for the yearly hunting and fishing. When Ray was at home with his mother and father, he talked about baseball, as he often did. The conversation moved to American League pitchers. Ray brought up Yankees hurler Carl Mays and his propensity to hit batters, adding quickly that it did not bother him because he knew how to get out of the way. It was just casual conversation, but the words would be remembered for a lifetime by all present in the house.

While in Kentucky he stopped to visit his longtime friend John Reid Alexander, who owned a large collection of phonograph records, particularly those of John McCormack, the world-famous Irish tenor. McCormack had recently appeared at a Cleveland theater before an enthusiastic crowd of 3,000 fans. He received rave notices in all of the Cleveland papers.

One of McCormack's songs was playing when Ray walked into the house. There were several guests in the home who did not know Ray personally, giving Alexander a great opportunity for a practical joke. He looked up in surprise and said, "As I live it is my old friend John McCormack himself! Friends I have a great treat in store for you. You have been listening to songs on the machine by McCormack. Well, here is McCormack in person." Ray, always up for a good prank, told Alexander he only had the old songs, so why not get some new ones for him to sing? Apparently that was as far as he wanted to take the charade. Alexander pushed the impostor to sing an old tune. Ray claimed he only knew "In the Shade of the Old Apple Tree" but managed to croon his best tenor impression, which satisfied everybody in attendance. The next day Alexander was overwhelmed with local requests for John McCormack to sing at nearby schools and societies. For the rest of the visit Ray kept up a low profile; no more singing for him until safely out of town.

Now that a sense of normalcy had been restored, the 1919 spring training at New Orleans had an air of determination about it. Last's year's second-place finish had raised the bar for the club, which now had valid expectations of a pennant, the first for the Indians since the American League started play in 1901. In early March Jim Dunn pulled the trigger on a major trade, sending outfielder Bobby Roth to the Philadelphia Athletics for three players: third baseman Larry Gardner, outfielder Charlie Jamieson, and pitcher Elmer Myers. The veteran Gardner had played in three World Series in his time with Boston, while Jamieson would have the opportunity to compete for the left field job. The infield now had returning vet Doc Johnston, Wamby, Ray, and Gardner. The outfield featured Speaker in center; power-hitting Elmer Smith in right field with Joe Wood backing him up (Wood, who had suffered for years from a chronically sore arm, had made a successful transition from pitcher to outfielder); and Jack Graney, Joe Evans, and Jamieson competing for the one open spot in left. Bagby and Coveleski anchored the pitching staff.

Though the players worked hard, knowing they had an opportunity to contend, there were a few occasions for fun and games. On March 28 Ray and team trainer Percy Smallwood squared off for a match race, two complete laps around the entire baseball field. Smallwood was a champion middle-distance runner, but Ray had great sprinter speed.

By race time $100 in bets between the players had been taken. Ray came out of the clubhouse in track shorts and running shoes, resolved to win his side bet of $20. On the signal to start, the runners set off at a fast pace through the first lap. They were even in lap two, but with a hundred feet to go Ray kicked in his finishing gear, flying by Smallwood to win the race in an unofficial time of one minute, forty-seven seconds. The players who cashed in their bets believed Ray was without question the fastest man in baseball and were already planning to run him against Max Carey of the Pirates for a winner-take-all $500. The scheme died in spring training, but it would have been an interesting competition.

In the middle of April, Ray, Speaker, and several others were on the field getting themselves ready for the regular work-out when somebody smelled smoke coming from the Pelicans clubhouse. The small group dashed inside, where they found the woodstove on fire. They were able to find some buckets, fill them with water, and douse the fire before it got out of hand. Quick work by the amateur firemen probably saved the clubhouse and part of the grandstand from ruin. The boys made their way back to the diamond to resume their warm-ups as if nothing had happened. Just a regular practice day at the ballpark.

Near the end of camp Ray, Speaker, and Graney played a spirited round of golf, with Speaker shooting a respectable 90, Ray a decent 92, and Graney, possibly using a bat, an astounding 115. Golf was becoming more and more popular with ballplayers. In years to come, the golf clubs and bats would be packed for the long trip north to prepare for the regular season.

Before leaving New Orleans, Ray had a few extra moments to relate another of his celebrated tall tales, this one about Jim Bagby. The event supposedly took place against the Yankees in 1917. Bagby had a 2–0 lead going into the ninth inning. He retired the first New York batter, then walked the next two. While Ray paced back and forth at shortstop, the Indians pitcher promptly hit the next batter. Disgusted, Ray called for time and walked to the mound. He told Bagby, "You call yourself a pitcher? Here we stake you to a lead of two runs and you quit like a dog?" Bagby looked at his annoyed shortstop and answered in his best southern drawl, "Chappie, they ain't scored on me yet." The game resumed with Frank "Home Run" Baker at the plate. Bagby delivered and the third baseman hit a one-hopper to Ray. He threw to Steve O'Neill, who stepped on home plate then fired to first to get Baker for the double play.

Cleveland won the game 2–0 and Bagby strolled back to the dugout for the usual handshakes and slaps on the back. When Ray marched by, the winning pitcher smiled and said, "Didn't I tell you Chappie that they hadn't scored off me yet?"

Cleveland's final tune-up before the start of the regular season was a three-game series with the Milwaukee Brewers in Evansville, Indiana. Ray's entourage from Owensboro had chartered an excursion boat, the *Golden Girl,* to carry 150 of his friends to downtown Evansville. Another 50 booked passage via railroad.

In game one Ray did not disappoint his crowd, scoring three runs while recording two hits and a steal in the 8–2 win. In the series he banged out seven hits in twelve trips to the plate. After the final game the Indians boarded a train for Michigan. The season was to begin at Detroit on April 23. A rather late start, but the major leagues wanted to allow the returning war veterans some extra time to get ready. Unfortunately, rain and wind postponed the game and the next day's contest as well.

On Friday, in spite of wet grounds and heavy wind gusts, the opener was played in front of a sparse crowd of 8,000. The Tigers were leading 3–1 in the seventh inning with runners on first and third when Ty Cobb hit a high pop fly to left center field. Graney and Speaker were both in position to make the play, but Ray waved them off. He circled under the high flier, but a blast of wind sent the ball on a downward path toward the infield. Ray stumbled forward to make the catch but slipped on the wet grass, landing on his backside while the baseball dropped in front of him. A run scored and the Tigers got the victory, 4–2.

Thus the season began, a year when major changes would affect Ray both on the ballfield and in his personal life. He now wore custom-made shirts to go with his freshly pressed suits, always appearing well-groomed in public. Some of the players called him the Beau Brummell of the American League. For the season he rented a comfortable seven-room apartment on

East Seventieth Street, four blocks from League Park, rather than a cramped rooming house with few amenities.

Ray began to pay income tax, complaining to his family about the $85 going to the government that year. His salary had not increased significantly, but the rate of taxation had escalated as a means for Washington to pay the vast expenses related to World War I. In 1913, when income tax was initiated for all Americans, Ray's bracket paid only 1 percent. With a few exemptions, he and most ballplayers could pay little or nothing. However, the inevitability of financial change had arrived, and with it baseball players were now forced to ante up.

His engagement to Katy was now in its third year, with seemingly no remaining obstacles in their path to keep the two apart. The matter of finances and a suitable place to live still loomed, but the time had arrived for Ray and Katy to walk down the aisle. No official announcements were made during the summer schedule, but plans were in motion for a most elaborate fall wedding that Clevelanders would chatter about for years.

A MARRIED MAN

The home opener took place on May 1 at League Park under cloudy skies and the constant threat of rain. After the customary display of pomp and circumstance, 16,000 fans watched silently as Detroit pounded the would-be pennant contenders, 8–1. Ray started the year without any fireworks, but by midmonth he warmed up considerably. In a home game with the Senators he singled twice and scored two times in the early going. He saved the best for later. In the eighth inning, with Jim Bagby on first, he belted a drive that bounced to the base of the left center field wall. He electrified the crowd by galloping around the bases so quickly that he almost caught Bagby on the way home, and crossed the plate without a throw. The final tally showed three hits, three runs scored, and two RBIs in the 11–2 blowout.

A triple play is a rare accomplishment, but in early June the Indians pulled off an especially unusual one. It happened at home against the St. Louis Browns. In the top of the fourth inning George Sisler led off with an infield base hit. Bill "Baby Doll" Jacobson reached on an error, then right fielder Tod Sloan bunted safely past the pitcher's mound to load the bases.

Wally Gerber, the Browns shortstop, lifted a fly ball to Joe Wood in right field. Sisler tagged up and scored easily, but an alert Ray cut off the throw home and fired the ball to third baseman Larry Gardner, trapping Jacobson between second and third. While Gardner chased Jacobson back to second, Ray hustled over to cover third. In the meantime, Sloan thought he could take second, but the throw from Gardner to Wamby arrived in time to retire the runner for the second out. Noticing Jacobson still a long way from third, Wamby threw to Ray to once again trap the stranded runner. In a textbook rundown, Ray chased him back toward second, then tossed to Wamby. In an instant the Cleveland second baseman tracked down the Browns center fielder and applied the tag for out number three and the triple play. It was a scorer's nightmare to record the three outs, but the heady play from the three infielders brought the Cleveland fans to their feet. Cleveland won the game, 6–3.

On or about June 19 Ray injured his lower back. The papers called it an attack of the lumbago. He tried to play through it but had to sit for an extended period. Taking his place was Harry Lunte, a first-year player who started off hitting like Ty Cobb until the American League pitchers figured him out. Without Ray in the everyday lineup, the Indians slumped over the next few weeks, winning less than half their ballgames. Dr. Castle believed the back injury would take until August to heal, much too long as far as the team's pennant aspirations. Whether he was healthy or not, Ray made a relief appearance on July 10 and returned as a starter on July 13. At the time Cleveland sported a record of 41–32, leaving them in third place, five and a half games behind the Chicago White Sox.

On July 18 the Red Sox and Indians met at League Park. It was a seesaw contest, but in the eighth Cleveland scored four runs to take a 7–3 lead. Boston scored once in the ninth, then, with the bases full and two outs, Babe Ruth launched a rocket far over the right field wall. The game was lost 8–7, and so was manager Lee Fohl's tenure with the Indians. By the end of the day a new player-manager, Tris Speaker, took charge of the team.

The next afternoon 10,000 fans were in the seats to see the debut of the new leader. They were thrilled with the change as the Indians won handily, 7–4. Ray seemed to respond with his best friend now his boss, lashing two triples and scoring twice. Usually a player elevated to manager puts some distance between himself and his friends on the club. It is extremely difficult to be a comrade and manager at the same time with everybody on the club trying to win favor from him. However, the relationship between Speaker and Chapman went on just as before. They continued to pal around, and in two months Speaker would accept an important heartfelt request from Ray.

The change of manager paid major dividends for the course of Cleveland baseball history. The players picked up the pace, overtaking the Yankees for second place in early August. Ray's batting average improved from .291 in July to .314 by mid-August. He was red hot at the plate, knocking out doubles and triples and driving in runs. From July 19 to the end of the month he had posted an eleven-game hitting streak, over which he batted .462 with 12 runs scored. The ascension of Speaker to manager fired up Ray to beyond his usual ultracompetitive nature. He always wanted to win badly, but even more so for the new skipper.

The lowly Philadelphia Athletics were in town for an August 24 matchup. Pitcher Ray Caldwell, just signed as a free agent by Cleveland, got the starting assignment. Throughout the afternoon distant sounds of thunder were heard, with an occasional flash of lightning. In the top of the ninth Caldwell was ready to put the finishing touches on a well-pitched 2–1 game. Suddenly a tremendous flash of lightning exploded on the grounds, knocking down Caldwell and sending shocks through the spikes of the players on the field. At shortstop Ray felt something go through his leg, leaving it completely numb for several minutes. He dragged himself to the mound along with the other infielders, fearing the worst had happened to their new pitcher. But not only did Caldwell survive, he finished the game! If the guys could make it through a direct blast of lightning, surely the gods were in their favor.

At the end of August the first-place Chicago White Sox came to League Park for a weekend series. Though the Sox owned an eight-game lead over the Indians, Saturday's contest drew 20,000 fans to League Park. In the bottom of the third with the bases loaded, Ray slashed a single to drive in the game's first two runs. He had three hits for the afternoon, keeping his average above .300 in the 4–0 win. On Sunday he laid down four sacrifice bunts as the home team rolled to a 6–1 victory. The series left them six games out of the first with a month to play, which proved to be a tad too much ground to make up in September.

Ray had a few more highlights left in him before the conclusion of the season. Playing against Philadelphia in the first game of a doubleheader, Ray put on his running shoes, swiping four bases in an 8–2 victory. Five days later in Washington, in the top of the fifth inning he thrilled the fans by sending a drive down into the left field corner. He sped around second base and gained momentum as he circled around third. The relay throw from the shortstop to the catcher was not in time as Ray slid hard across home plate. The 8–4 win made it ten in a row for the surging Indians, still clinging to a chance to overtake the White Sox.

With four games left in the season, the Indians stopped in Detroit for two games. When the Tigers won the first game, Cleveland was finally eliminated from the race for first but had clinched second, while the Tigers were still scuffling with the Red Sox for a third-place finish and with it a share of the World Series money. With nothing for the Indians to play for, Speaker told Ray to skip the next day's contest. He even allowed him to catch an immediate train to Cleveland to visit Katy. They would meet up again Saturday at League Park for the final two games against St. Louis.

Detroit won the last game of the series, 9–5, without much fight from the Cleveland side. Seven years later, in 1926, Speaker, Ty Cobb, and Joe Wood faced an accusation from Dutch Leonard, the pitcher for Detroit on Wednesday, that they had fixed the Thursday game to allow the Tigers to have a chance to finish third. Leonard's claim was strong enough for Commissioner Landis to schedule a hearing in early 1927.

Immediately, Cobb's lawyer tried to spin things, arguing Cleveland's loss was due to Ray's absence. He summed it up to romance being responsible. The attorney stated Ray was, "playing his head off all season" and his being out of town resulted in Speaker innocently telling Leonard that Detroit would win the next day.

Inadvertently, Cobb's lawyer opened up a can of worms. He let Judge Landis's office know Ray was missing for the alleged betting and game throwing. It could be inferred that the accused were aware Ray would not stand for his team laying down. If Landis pursued this line of thinking, how would the defense counter it?

Ray's substitute, Harry Lunte, had not seen much playing time and did not show particularly well, booting two chances. Lunte's addition to the lineup seemed to aid Leonard's allegations, which were bolstered by several incriminating letters sent among the trio.

The Speaker-Cobb-Wood defense benefited from the absence of key witnesses. Ray was no longer alive in 1926, and for unspecified reasons Dutch Leonard failed to appear at the scheduled hearing. Without Leonard, Commissioner Landis dismissed the case. Though Cobb and Speaker were free to play ball in 1927 (Wood had retired several years ago), the legitimacy of the August 1919 game still remains suspect.

Under player-manager Speaker the ball club finished 1919 with a record of 84–55, their best effort percentage-wise since 1908. Finishing in second place gave the Cleveland players a World Series share for the second year in a row. Ray, despite missing twenty-five games, managed to hit .300 for the third time in his career. The errors still came at inopportune moments, but he continued to excel in his overall play, still laying claim to be the elite shortstop in the American League.

Putting the baseball season behind him, Ray steadied himself for the biggest moment of his twenty-nine years. He had made the long, difficult journey from a small town in Kentucky all the way to the big leagues in Cleveland. But even that could not totally prepare him for what awaited. On October 29, 1919, in Cleveland, Raymond Johnson Chapman would marry Kathleen Marie Daly in an elaborate afternoon ceremony at the Dalys' splendid Euclid Avenue home.

The wedding was without a doubt one of the most anticipated events of northeast Ohio in recent memory. Of all the many noteworthy weddings in the region, none had the appeal of one of baseball's great stars and the most desirable woman for miles around. It made great copy for the papers and a fertile topic for gossipmongers. All three local newspapers, the *Plain Dealer, News,* and the *Press,* had reporters geared up for extensive coverage on the sports pages along with the exceedingly popular society pages.

The October wedding for Ray meant a short trip home to Herrin then a return date to Cleveland to be the guest of honor at his high-profile bachelor party. In between he squeezed in a trip to Chicago to catch one of the World Series games between the White Sox and the Cincinnati Reds. Ray, like many others, witnessed several questionable home team plays on the field. Within a year eight members of the Sox would be suspended for life by Commissioner Landis for allegedly throwing Series games. Among the fallen was Joe Jackson, although the debate about his guilt or innocence still continues.

For Katy, several weeks of nonstop elegant bridal parties and luncheons were scheduled to celebrate her transition from single girl into the world of marriage. Many of Cleveland's privileged families anxiously waited for the postman to deliver the coveted wedding invitation, sent to several hundred homes. Tuxedos and evening gowns would need to be cleaned and pressed and new designs appropriate for the fall purchased.

With the wedding less than a month away, Martin Daly finalized his plans to welcome Ray to the Daly family and another way of life. His new son-in-law had proven to be a man of high character, more than suitable to marry his daughter. Ray had money in the bank along with war bonds earning interest, but he would need much more to give Katy the life she wanted. Here Mr. Daly stepped up in a big way.

Soon after the marriage and honeymoon took place, Ray would start a new job as secretary-treasurer of the Pioneer Brass and Alloy Company. Daly was not quite a kingmaker, but he had the power and influence to secure his soon-to-be son-in-law a highly placed executive post. Ray could not have been qualified for such a job, but it was his to learn and hold onto while collecting a salary not in the same hemisphere as his baseball contract. With stock options likely attached, Ray would have the means to support his wife in the style she was accustomed to.

Ray delighted in taking his friends to see the company and giving them a tour of the facilities. Steve O'Neill remembered stopping in the doorway of the new secretary-treasurer. Ray laughed and told him, "See that desk? I'll have my feet upon that and you and some of those other ball players will be out in that hot boiler factory sweating and tugging at big pieces of brass!"

There are many accounts that Ray planned to continue to play ball or retire from baseball while fulfilling his duties at Pioneer Brass. According to which newspaper one read, he loved playing baseball and wanted to keep at it, or he would play until the Indians won a pennant, hopefully in 1920. Without question his father-in-law wanted him to work full-time and help Katy raise a family, but Ray's real intentions were never made clear. The Indians were a ball club with the talent to win it all, and a first-place finish in a year or two remained a distinct possibility. That way he could satisfy his baseball ambitions as well as his rising family responsibilities.

In addition to a high-paying job, Martin had other plans for his daughter and son-in-law. He and his wife, Kathleen (Katy's mother), bought ample land on Alvason Road in East Cleveland, a few blocks from the Daly home. The property was deeded to Katy only, with an interesting clause stating, "No intoxicating liquors shall be manufactured on property." Perhaps Cuyahoga County was getting a head start on Prohibition. On site a stylish brick home would be constructed as a wedding present for the couple, with eleven rooms, including three bedrooms, and a finished third floor to lodge a housekeeper or nanny. A two-car garage would be built on the property, with adjacent space for a large formal garden. The Dalys could easily walk to the Alvason home for visits and dinners and later get acquainted with the ordained conclusion of many grandchildren.

Ray was thrilled to have a grand house to call his own. For all of his adult years he had lived in rooming houses, apartments, and hotels while wintering with his parents in Herrin along with his uncle in Owensboro. Being a single ballplayer gave him the lifestyle of a nomad, constantly packing a suitcase for another destination. In the course of the season there were seven different cities to visit, then time in Herrin, off to Owensboro, a trip to Cleveland to see his fiancée, and back to Herrin. That way of life would give way to a sole location on Alvason Road, at least for October through February and year-round once Ray retired from baseball. While in Cleveland, he made frequent trips to the construction site to watch the house take shape, bringing along many of his friends and instructing them on the fine points of building a home. Steve O'Neill recalled believing Ray knew every brick and its place on the property. All you had to do was ask him.

Martin Daly had taken great pains to see that his daughter had the capital for a dazzling start to the marriage, including a lovely home and a husband with an executive position. Winter vacations to the West Coast and trips to Europe were within easy reach, as were Katy's ambitions to entertain and play a major role in Cleveland's high society. The two of them seemed bound for a fairytale life.

In mid-October the wedding festivities began with a two-week schedule of well-planned parties for the bride. The Daly family's many friends and associates got in line for the opportunity to host one of the events. On October 15 a large reception at Cleveland's Opera House was held for Katy. The following day an extravagant tea party took place on East Ninety-Seventh Street, an exclusive neighborhood, followed by a luncheon the next day on the very same street.

A few days later another luncheon was held at the select Chagrin Valley Hunt Club, hosted by a recently married friend of Katy's, then an afternoon affair at the very private Shaker Heights Country Club. Dorothy Barrett hosted this, a bridesmaid and college student who traveled home from college just to throw the luncheon for her dear friend. On Sunday, October 26, the receptions moved east of Cleveland to the Willowick Country Club for an evening including a sumptuous dinner. By now Katy needed a sizable truck to haul all the wedding gifts presented to her. The celebrations ended two days before the nuptials with yet another luncheon at the Cleveland Heights home of an additional bridesmaid.

Ray finally got his turn at the bachelor party, hosted by Tris Speaker. The bash took place at the classy Hotel Winton on Prospect Avenue just east of Ninth Street. Thirty guests attended, including Jack Graney and most of the Indians, as well as champion boxer Johnny Kilbane and people from Owensboro and New York City. The hotel featured top-shelf Italian food prepared by in-house master and soon-to-be famous Chef Boiardi.

Speaker and several other friends went in on a large wedding gift purchased in New York City. The present, likely a heavy piece of furniture, was too bulky to be sent by mail or fit in someone's auto, so a New York friend, an army major, bought two seats for it on a drawing room car on the New York Central Railroad.

The wedding announcement was a front-page story in the *Sporting News.* Under a photo of Ray, the caption read in part, "The joy of Herrin, Illinois is tempered with sorrow. Ray Chapman of the Cleveland Indians is going to be married. The bride is a Cleveland girl and that means Chapman will say good-bye to Herrin and hereafter make his home in the Ohio City." Katy, said the caption, was "one of the most handsome and accomplished young ladies in the Sixth City [Cleveland]."

Mr. and Mrs. Chapman and their children arrived from Herrin for the wedding, staying as guests at the Daly home. The Dalys and Chapmans were miles apart socially, a coal miner's family and the family of the head of the East Ohio Gas Company. Up to this point they had had little contact with each other, but now it was unavoidable, awkward as their interactions might be.

The afternoon ceremony would be officiated by Father Joseph Smith, the head of St. Philomena Church in East Cleveland. Father Smith, a friend of John D. Rockefeller, had maintained a personal friendship with the Daly family since their arrival in Cleveland many years ago. As a gesture to his dear friends, and to spare Ray and his family any uncomfortable moments, he agreed to marry Ray and Katy away from the church at a nondenominational site, the Dalys' home. Apparently the Chapmans were supportive of Ray's decision to marry a Catholic, fully embracing Ray's choice of Katy and any religious concerns that might arise. The Dalys, particularly Martin, had some reservations, but for the time being he put them aside, believing there would be a place later on for discussion.

An hour before the wedding a large parade of autos converged on Euclid Avenue and East 135th Street. The guests filled the spacious home, looking for the best vantage point to see the bride and groom. Soon Ray walked confidently down the aisle, accompanied by his best man, Tris Speaker. The ushers lined up, including Walter Daly, the eldest of the Daly sons. Moments later the bridesmaids appeared, wearing beautiful gowns of rainbow-hued taffeta with hats of gold lace, led by maid of honor Jane McMahon. Mrs. Daly wore black velvet with a train, while Ray's mom had on black satin with gold embroidery.

After a minute or two, all in attendance turned to see the bride walk slowly down the aisle escorted by her proud father. Katy wore a dazzling wedding gown of ivory satin and duchess lace with a train of embroidered pearls. Her lace veil had a small Juliet cap (named for the Shakespeare heroine) with clusters of bright orange blossoms. Every detail had to be perfect, and it was.

Father Smith guided the two through the happy ceremony; they were now Mr. and Mrs. Ray Chapman for all the world to see. After a lengthy time for congratulations, the bride and groom adjourned to the Gilmour Council Club, a banquet hall recently built by the Knights of Columbus, just a few blocks away. The rooms were finely decorated with yellow mums on each table along with fresh autumn leaves. The guests soon followed, eagerly looking forward to an evening of fine dining and dancing.

By coincidence, the day before the wedding, Congress had ratified the Volstead Act, banning liquor sales throughout the country. Prohibition would not be enforced until the early months of 1920, however, allowing the Daly-Chapman celebration to be loaded with cases of the best champagne and finest liquor. Any booze purchased before the cutoff date could be used as long as the supply lasted, so if any alcohol remained at the end of the night it presumably went to the Daly home so they could begin stocking up.

To kick off the celebration, Mr. and Mrs. Daly plus Ray along with Katy danced the Virginia reel, a social dance of Scottish origin popular in the United States since the 1700s. The guests were then treated to a music recital by noted Irish tenor Frank Gafney, who sang the popular tune "Believe Me If All Those Endearing Young Charms." The evening went on with the newlyweds making the rounds of the tables and happily dancing until the early morning hours. The next day's *Cleveland News* carried the headline on the sports page, "If base hits ring from Chappie's bat in 1920 as wedding bells did Wednesday, Oh Boy!"

Early the next morning the couple packed their suitcases in Ray's car and headed off on their honeymoon. For several years Ray had eagerly wanted Katy to meet his mother's Owensboro relatives, and their first destination was Kentucky for a fancy luncheon reception. After a short visit they were on the road west for a stop in French Lick, Indiana, to stay at one of the most exclusive resorts in America. The area had an abundance of prized mineral water, believed to be therapeutic for just about any medical issues. A long, relaxing bath in the warm or cold waters was recommended for the thousands of guests who arrived from all parts of the States and beyond. The resort was a gathering place for the rich and famous: Hollywood stars, top musicians, politicians, and even the likes of Al Capone booked time there.

For Ray and Katy it was a great honeymoon adventure with two golf courses, horseback riding, tennis courts, bowling alleys, and spas with manicures and pedicures for the ladies. There were vapor and oxygen baths, with massages readily available. Vegetables were grown on the grounds and barnyards, and Holstein cows provided the freshest milk anywhere. It was an ideal place for sheer relaxation from the busy lifestyles they would resume upon their return home.

Once back in Cleveland, the Chapmans rented a house on Superior Avenue, where they would live during the baseball season until the Alvason Road home was ready to occupy. Ray began his responsibilities at Pioneer Brass, attempting to learn all the intricacies of the financial world in record time. He worked there until early March of 1920, then took Katy with him to spring training. On March 3 Ray and Katy met the Indians' train in Carbondale, Illinois, having stopped in Herrin first. Katy would not be the only woman at camp, as Jack Graney brought along his mother and sister the following day, so Katy would not be without female company.

The month in New Orleans served as an extension of the Chapmans' honeymoon. The southern city had its apportionment of fine restaurants, charming shops, and nightclubs on Bourbon Street or the racy French Quarter (if you dared). During the day Katy would sit in the bleachers at Pelican Park, watching her husband work himself into playing shape. Before long newspapers across the country picked up the local story about the immensely popular couple spending as much time together as possible. Anybody who saw them could not help but notice the deep-seated affection between the two.

In the first part of March, sports editor Robert Maxwell, reporting for a Philadelphia paper, was making the rounds of the major league camps and stopped in New Orleans. Maxwell saw the Indians as the team to beat in the American League and was most impressed with Ray and his fellow infielders, writing, "You can't pass up an infield like that for it looks like the class of the league. The men are seasoned veterans, playing a steady, brainy game."

Another paper described Ray as the "best shortstop in the business today. A great hitter one of the best baserunners in the game and a wonder in the field." The compliments were fine, but surely Ray would have traded them all for a first-place finish. Before he left Herrin for his wedding he had told the family this was the year for Cleveland to win the pennant. He promised older brother Roy, a devoted fan, box seats for all the World Series games at League Park.

This spring training was the first for Tris Speaker as player-manager. He tried to keep the team dynamic intact, socializing with the players as before. Before camp he came to Cleveland to visit Ray and Katy, made plans to room with Joe Wood as he had since their time in Boston, then squeezed in a hunting trip with backup catcher Les Nunamaker. During training there were several days of rainy weather, keeping everybody inside the De Soto Hotel. The thoughtful Tris bought bouquets of roses for Katy and several other wives who were disappointed at losing time to go sightseeing.

When the skies cleared, a national moving picture company visited the Cleveland players at practice. A cameraman took many photos and several film sequences, which unfortunately have not survived. One of those involved Ray laying down a bunt and beating the throw to first base. Ray's teammates told him he could give Charlie Chaplin a run for his money.

The high point of this year's camp was the game featuring the righties versus the lefties, with a box of cigars and dinner for the winning team. Ray served as captain for the right-handers, while former roommate Graney directed the "crooked arms." Each team had their share of batsmen, but while the Chapman squad featured pitchers Bagby, Coveleski, and Guy Morton, Graney's guys only had Ray Caldwell. Because of the likelihood of some hot-blooded moments, umpire and Indians coach Jack McAlister excused himself from working the game. Ray and Graney found an umpire from the Southern Association to call the ball and strikes, then collected money from the players to pay his fee.

Using his pitchers wisely, Ray and his righties won the game, 5–1. Afterwards the lefties, trying to salvage something, bragged about being able to engineer three double plays to the righties' none. Ray answered, "You can't make double plays when there is no one on the bases!" That response silenced the losers, who grudgingly accepted the defeat and the lack of cigars or a grand dinner.

Near the end of the month the *Sporting News* reported that the New Orleans Pelicans had signed standout University of Alabama shortstop Joe Sewell. The paper noted that the owner of the Pelicans happened to be none other than Charles Somers. No binding agreement existed between the ball clubs, but Cleveland usually received the first choice of anyone on the Pelicans roster. If infield help were needed during the 1920 season and beyond, Sewell would be available to the Indians.

On April 13 the Chapmans' marathon honeymoon ended with Katy taking the train to Cleveland to temporarily stay with her parents. The *Plain Dealer's* society pages listed a number of women who would be attending the opener, and Mrs. Chapman's name was at the top.

The next day nearly 20,000 fans packed the stands at League Park, the majority wearing heavy coats with gloves and scarves. The usual bands were there, with U.S. Marines smartly raising the grand old flag in center field. Because of the cold, many of the fans were yelling, "Play ball!" halfway through the ceremonies. They waited impatiently for Mayor Harry Davis to hurry up and throw the first ball and for all the officials on the field to shake hands then quickly get out of the way.

The 1920 edition of the Cleveland Indians trotted to their positions with the highest expectations in franchise history. They had been knocking on the door for two years, and many sportswriters across the country believed the time had come for a pennant. Manager Speaker's roster was loaded with superb talent in the hitting and pitching departments. Still the preeminent defensive center fielder in baseball and one of the game's best hitters, he had fine batsmen in Ray, Larry Gardner, Elmer Smith, and Steve O'Neill. Speaker loved to platoon his ballplayers and would sub in Joe Wood, Joe Evans, and Jack Graney in the outfield depending on who was pitching for the opposition. He also had Bill Wamby and Doc Johnston starting. The lineup was overflowing with ability.

On the pitching side were Stan Coveleski and Jim Bagby along with veterans Ray Caldwell and Guy Morton as the starters. Though they could have used another arm, what they had would carry them a long way. Jim Dunn had given Speaker the pieces he needed to bring home the first flag to Cleveland since the American League began play in 1901. The lineup for opening day was as follows:

> Graney lf
> Chapman ss
> Speaker cf
> Smith rf
> Gardner 3b
> Wamby 2b
> Johnston 1b
> O'Neill c
> Coveleski p

LOVE AND LOSS

Graney would be replaced at the end of May by Charlie Jamieson along with Joe Evans in left field. Other than Joe Wood subbing for Elmer Smith, the core of the starters played every day. Ray had the dual responsibility of moving along the runner or getting on base for Speaker and Smith. At this stage in his career he was more than capable of doing both.

Despite the wintry conditions, the Indians scored four times in the second inning to coast to a 5–0 win over the St. Louis Browns. Ray collected two base hits while stealing his first base of the year. With his private life in fine order, he could devote all his energies to assisting in the struggle for the pennant.

On Sunday the eighteenth Ray demonstrated what an expert ballplayer can do for a team's fortunes. An overflow crowd of 23,307 watched the shortstop slash a double to drive in a run and score three runs himself in an 11–4 rout of the Tigers. In addition, he displayed a combination of speed and smarts in scoring from third on a shallow fly off the bat of Joe Wood. In the sixth inning Wood lifted a high pop fly to right field, where second baseman Ralph Young drifted back to make the catch. Ray, standing nonchalantly on third base, waited a split second before dashing for home. The astonished Young took an extra instant to get the ball out of his glove and hurried his throw wide of the plate while Ray slid home with ease. Like few others in the game, Ray seemed to always know when he could catch somebody snoozing and take advantage of the moment.

By early May it was evident Ray was off to a special season. In a road game with the champion 1919 White Sox, with the score tied 2–2 in the top of the tenth inning, he lined a single to drive in the go-head run. Jim Bagby held on in the bottom of the tenth to win 3–2 and move to within a half game of first place. Ray, along with eight of his teammates, carried a batting average over .300.

Three days later Cleveland led Chicago 2–0 heading into the visitors' half of the ninth inning. Graney walked and Ray bunted to the side of the mound, where pitcher Eddie Cicotte fielded the ball and threw it away. The runners advanced to second and third, and each scored on a sacrifice fly. The White Sox came back with three runs in the bottom half, but the scoring ended with Cleveland holding on, 4–3. The 3–1 series win vaulted them into first place over the Red Sox and White Sox, a foreshadowing of what was to come. It was still May and the schedule had over a hundred games to play, but the boys who played at League Park were flashing signs of a true championship ball club.

Later in the month the Indians were at Shibe Park taking on the A's. Umpires George Hildebrand and Billy Evans made several tough calls against the home team. In a time-honored tradition, at the end of the game several hundred vengeful fans climbed the railing, blocking the path to the visitors' dugout. The two umpires were trapped on the field with no escape. Manager Speaker jumped in front of the mob with Ray next to him waving a bat. Several more players joined the two, followed by most of the Athletics. They shoved the crowd back until Hildebrand and Evans could make their escape. Almost forgotten was the score, 4–1, in favor of Cleveland.

With Cleveland playing inspired baseball, the *Plain Dealer* ran a series of cartoons featuring members of the club, including a lifelike sketch of Ray standing to the left of second base as if waiting for a throw. The caption to another cartoon read, "Fastest Man in the American League," with a cloud of smoke nearby and a caricature of a catcher wiping his brow, saying, "Gosh! Greased Lightning!" The cartoon was not far from the truth. Ray was living up to his press clippings, batting over .300 and scoring runs at a rapid pace while treating the home fans to some highlight reel moments in the field.

Life for Ray Chapman was at its absolute zenith. He was playing the best ball of his career and enjoying a marriage filled with happiness and the blissful news of a child on the way in early 1921. Ray had to be walking on air. Some time ago he had told reporters, "I like the kids and I want them all for my

friends. For me, no affection can equal that of the little folks."
As proof he would nick practice balls from League Park and
toss them to children waiting outside. If having a baby was not
enough to celebrate, the splendid house on Alvason stood to
be ready for a move-in by early October. All the boxes were
checked for the Chapmans to relish the years ahead.

In mid-June the Yankees came calling for four games at
League Park. Ruth and company were tied with the Indians
for the American League lead. The Indians took the opener
5–4, then absorbed a 14–0 massacre in game two. New York
had eighteen hits, with six of the nine batters getting two or
more. While the Indians licked their wounds in the clubhouse,
Ray stood up and spoke loudly enough for all the reporters to
hear. He said, "We'll get 'em sure tomorrow and next day!" His
teammates reportedly grunted in agreement, doubtless using
words the writers could not print. Whether Ray's short speech
spurred them on or not, Cleveland smoked the Yankees in the
next two contests, 7–1 and 10–2.

In the series the Indians shortstop continued his exceptional play, recording four hits, scoring four times, including
the winning run in the opener, walking five times, and stealing
a base. New York left town in second place, trailing Cleveland
by two full games. Ray moved a step closer to realizing his goal
of a World Series, trying to grab the brass ring in two different
worlds.

10 TRAGEDY AT THE POLO GROUNDS

As the season wound its way to August, Ray was putting up remarkable offensive numbers. At the end of June at Comiskey Park he had played the one thousandth game of his major league career, the longest-tenured player on the current Cleveland roster. The *Sporting News* reported that he had recently reached the 1,000-hit plateau. His batting average as of July 28 stood at .322 with 89 runs scored, second to only Babe Ruth, and 119 hits. He led the American League in sacrifices with 34, well on his way to leading the league again. At this pace he would have another 100-run season easily within reach along with a career-high batting average.

His steals were down considerably, but that can be largely attributed to Tris Speaker's new offensive philosophy. The manager believed he had the batters to concentrate on the hit-and-run rather than swiping bases. With guys in the lineup like Speaker, Elmer Smith, and Larry Gardner, Ray held his base rather than attempting his usual steals. The results indicated Speaker had a good thing going with a first-place team and plenty of runs scored.

Though holding onto first place by three games, the Indians had to play the Yankees seven times over the next month, four at home and three on the road. They began August in style, winning games with smart baserunning and timely hitting. Against Washington at home on August 3, Ray singled, Speaker walked, and Elmer Smith flied out to right field, Ray advancing to third. Ray and Speaker had noted that the Senators pitcher, Tom Zachary, took a long windup, and on the first pitch to Larry Gardner, Speaker raced for second while Ray dashed home. Startled, Zachary balked while attempting to throw the ball to his catcher, and Ray scored the first run of a 10–5 win.

In spite of his all-around good play, Ray still committed a few gaffes on the ballfield. The next day, with Charlie Jamieson on base, Ray laid down his nearly automatic sacrifice bunt. The Washington pitcher, Eric Erickson, picked up the ball and looked to second, then hesitated before throwing to first. Thinking he was a sure out, Ray did not run at full speed. If he had, he would likely have beaten the throw. Speaker was then hit by a pitch, which meant the bases would have been loaded and nobody out. With Smith and Gardner due to hit, it might have been a big inning, but no runs were scored.

On August 6 at League Park, Cleveland led 1–0 with the Athletics coming to bat in the top of the ninth. With one out, the A's hitter, Frank Welch, grounded to Ray, who fired the ball past a lunging Doc Johnston, allowing Welch to reach second base. Jimmy Dykes grounded to Ray; this time the throw was on the mark for out number two. But Tillie Walker then singled to drive in the run, tying the score at 1–1. The Indians failed to answer in the bottom half, sending the game to extra innings. Several writers in the press box noted that the game time after nine innings was only sixty-nine minutes, the fastest playing time of the season. Had Ray not made the error, the contest might well have gone into the record books. As it was, Philadelphia scored in the top of the tenth and got the victory, 2–1.

A day before the Yankees came to town, Ray went 2 for 3 against the A's, driving in a run and scoring one. In the seventh inning with Cleveland in front 2–0, his single drove in run number three. Jack Graney singled, sending Ray to third. The two old roommates quickly nodded to each other, then took off running when pitcher Herb Perry began his windup. The successful double steal raised the score to 4–0 in an eventual 5–0 triumph.

The Yankees came to Cleveland trailing the home team by four and one half games. Here was a chance for Ray and his teammates to assert themselves and leave the New Yorkers in the dust. Manager Miller Huggins told reporters he was apprehensive about facing Cleveland, mentioning Ray and Speaker as the two ballplayers he feared most. But, despite the huge partisan crowds at League Park, the visitors unexpectedly swept the series, leaving only a half game between the clubs. Ray had only three hits in the series, including 0 for 5 in the second game against the Yankees' Carl Mays. But though the hitting wasn't there, he played exceptional defense, including handling twenty-one of twenty-two chances cleanly in the first two games.

In Friday's game four Mays came on in relief, retiring Ray one more time to make it 0 for 6 in two meetings. New York left town confident of their chances with three home games against Cleveland beginning on Monday August 16. The Indians would play two weekend games with St. Louis, then hop on a train for New York for the return match. On Sunday they rolled over the Browns with ease, 5–0, but in the eighth inning Ray fanned with two runners aboard, his last at bat at League Park until the Indians completed their eastern road trip.

That night Ray packed his traveling bags and loaded the car, then went with Katy to pick up Jack Graney at his rooming house. At a later date Graney would remember the day, which included a stop at the almost-ready Chapman home. The three of them inspected the rooms, and Graney recalled how happy and excited his best friends were about moving in by early fall. They drove to the train station, and Katy joined them in the rail car until the conductor's whistle. The couple parted with their usual warm smiles and waves, already eager for the road trip to end.

The train reached New York City early Monday morning, and the players headed to the Ansonia Hotel to get settled. Despite scattered showers and gray skies, 21,000 excited fans made

LOVE AND LOSS

their way to the Polo Grounds to witness the clash of the two pennant contenders. Among the crowd was a host of photographers representing the many New York papers.

The lineups for the critical game were as follows:

Jamieson lf	Ward 3b
Chapman ss	Peckinpaugh ss
Speaker cf	Ruth rf
Smith rf	Pratt 2b
Gardner 3b	Lewis lf
O'Neill c	Pipp 1b
Johnston 1b	Bodie cf
Wamby 2b	Ruel c
Coveleski p	Mays p

Coveleski and Mays were both already eighteen-game winners, closing in on twenty-win seasons. Each lineup featured strong hitting, with the Yankees' Babe Ruth leading the way with a colossal 42 home runs. In the top of the first Jamieson reached base and Ray followed with a sacrifice bunt. The Indians were unable to score, but in the second inning Steve O'Neill launched a home run for a 1–0 lead. In the third inning, with Jamieson on base, Ray attempted another bunt but popped the ball up for an easy double play.

The game moved to the fifth inning, showers still coming down sporadically. The skies were an ugly gray when Ray led off. Mays looked in for the sign, holding a wet, scuffed, and dirty baseball. He wound up and delivered the pitch in his unorthodox submarine style. The baseball sailed inward, curving directly toward Ray. He either froze or never saw the fastball, standing completely still while the sphere hurtled directly at his left temple. The impact made a loud crack and the ball rolled out in the direction of the pitcher's mound.

In an interview years later, Yankees catcher Muddy Ruel reflected on the ill-fated pitch. In less than a second he could see the ball on its trajectory directly at Ray's head. He recalled yelling to the batter to duck, but it all happened too fast. Ruel knew the spinning baseball trickling into fair territory was not the result of a bunt.

Regardless, Mays gathered it up and threw to Wally Pipp at first. But there was no runner racing on his way down the baseline. All eyes turned to home plate, where Ray slumped to the ground inside the batter's box. At the same instant, the ball-players and people in the stands had the sickening realization that the speeding baseball had not been bunted but had struck Ray squarely in the head.

Umpire Tommy Connolly whipped off his mask, turned to the grandstand, and pleaded for a doctor. Medical help came within a moment. It is not clear from the accounts if stimulants or plain water were used to revive him, but gradually Ray opened his eyes and struggled to raise himself to a sitting position.

Surrounded by his alarmed teammates, except for Larry Gardner, who could not bear to look, Ray attempted to stand up, but needed help in getting off the ground. With assistance he walked gingerly toward the infield on his way to the visitors' clubhouse behind the left field fence. Seeing him upright, the New York fans and everybody in the park breathed a collective sigh of relief.

The group of photographers had ample time to snap pictures of the accident and its aftermath. From the moment Ray went down to the time he arrived at the clubhouse, at least ten minutes elapsed. Whether the men made a joint decision to abstain because of the horrific scene or never developed the negatives is uncertain. If there are any pictures of the gruesome scene, they are not in circulation.

Ray got as far as the beginning of the outfield grass when he suddenly collapsed. Two of the Indians gently picked him up and carried him the remaining distance to the clubhouse. The Yankees team doctor and another physician from nearby

St. Lawrence Hospital were waiting to examine him. Seeing him unconscious with blood gushing out of his left ear, they immediately called for an ambulance for the half-mile trip to St. Lawrence.

Jack McAlister, the Cleveland bench coach, thought he heard an explosion when the ball collided with Ray. Seeing him sprawled in a heap on the ground, he thought he was already dead. According to McAlister, Carl Mays approached umpire Connolly, arguing that the ball had hit the end of Ray's bat, making it in play for an out, but Wally Pipp, knowing what really occurred, eased Mays away from the umpire and the Indians standing nearby. Noting the expressions on the Cleveland players' faces, McAlister feared that more than a few of them were ready to tear Mays apart. He made sure to stand in front of them, between home plate and the mound, ready to hold off the mob if he could.

Pipp thought Ray had set himself for one of May's slow curveballs. In a previous at bat he had swung and missed the sweeping curve, and now he may have believed another one was coming. Mays crossed him up with a high hard one, and Ray was unable to adjust in time. On countless occasions hitters are fooled by a pitch, standing flat-footed while the ball harmlessly goes by. But the results were far from harmless this time. Pipp added that the day was terribly overcast, making it difficult for batters to get a good look at the pitches coming their way.

F. C. Lane, the editor of *Baseball Magazine*, was in the press box watching the game with Brooklyn pitcher Al Mamaux, who had the day off. When Lane heard the sound he thought Ray had bunted the ball. Mamaux, a seasoned ballplayer, knew immediately what had taken place and told Lane that Ray had been struck in the head. The editor worked his way down to the visitors' clubhouse, where he was intercepted by Colonel Huston, the Yankees co-owner. Huston, a combat veteran of two different wars (he had been promoted to colonel in World War I), told Lane the prognosis did not look good, but hoped he was mistaken. Lane stuck around and waited for Carl Mays to appear in the Yankee locker room, hoping to get an exclusive on his thoughts about the incident. The two men did speak, but the words did little to help Mays out of an unenviable situation.

Fred Lieb, the esteemed baseball writer for several major New York newspapers and chairman of the New York chapter of the Baseball Writers Association, saw the game from the downstairs press box, some fifty feet behind home plate. In his memoirs, published in 1977, he recalled watching the incident with an unobstructed view. When the pitch struck Ray, Lieb said to himself, "Why didn't he react, duck, throw himself to the ground?" He believed that Ray saw the pitch but completely froze. Lieb's recollections are quite ghastly; he claims, for example, that Ray's left eye was completely out of its socket before he fell to the ground. Coming fifty-seven years after the fact, with no other account mentioning that, Lieb's version is unconvincing.

Lieb made a point of visiting the Cleveland players before the next game they played, on Wednesday. He noted the bitterness each one expressed. He claimed that first baseman Doc Johnston, a southerner, went as far as saying Mays should be lynched for what he did. Only Speaker looked at the situation objectively, telling Lieb there was time for Ray to bail but he could not get out of the path of the ball. Batters were trained to get out of the way on tight inside pitches, he said, but somehow his shortstop, on this one occasion, never moved an inch.

As for Carl Mays, Lieb was blunt. He mentioned his and Dutch Leonard's long-standing reputation as beanball artists from their 1915–18 stints with the Boston Red Sox. Apparently manager Bill Carrigan had no concern about his pitchers throwing high and inside at any given time. Whether deservedly or not, many ballplayers in the American League considered Mays a bona fide headhunter.

Over the years, hundreds of varying accounts of the incident would be published. Some stories give Mays a free pass, saying he was just trying to move the hitter further off the plate, while others condemn him as a cold-blooded individual who cared little about another man's life. Because of the time period there is no audio to be reviewed or film to watch from every conceivable angle to assess the pitch. All that is known for certain is that the ball came at Ray at great speed and he could not duck or move his upper body to avoid the ball. It is left for all those interested to make their own judgment of Mays's intent.

It may have been an attempt to get quoted in the newspapers, but John Henry, Ray's friend from the Hawaii trip and former American League catcher, claimed to have been in the clubhouse before the ambulance arrived. Henry told reporters that Ray briefly whispered to him not to blame Mays for the errant pitch. It's unlikely a man with a severe head injury could speak; however, Henry seemed to be genuine. If somehow true, Ray must be considered for sainthood.

Even with the chilling incident on the field, the game had to resume. Cleveland scored again, upping their lead to 4–0. The Yankees rallied for three runs in the ninth but came up short, losing the important game 4–3. The Indians players showered and dressed quickly and left for the hospital to check on their friend. Manager Speaker and traveling secretary Walter McNicholls were the first to arrive and confer with the doctors. X-rays had been taken to check for a skull fracture, but the surgeons were optimistic the results would be negative, meaning an undetermined hospital stay but without any complicated treatment.

Speaker took a moment to phone the Cleveland papers to issue a statement on Ray's condition. He said, "I was hit in the head in 1916 in a manner similar to this and I am hopeful that Chappie will be back as soon as I was. I was badly scared when I saw Ray try to talk this afternoon, but he was able to talk tonight, so that worry was over."

Speaker also phoned the Daly home to reach Katy to explain what had happened to her husband. Considerably alarmed, she quickly packed a bag and left with Jane McMahon, who was in town visiting the family, for the Cleveland train station. Jane and the pregnant Katy boarded the 8:30 train for the overnight ride to New York City. It must have been the most difficult ride of her life.

While the players lingered at St. Lawrence for the results of Ray's X-rays, their thoughts turned toward a similar incident during spring training. Brooklyn and New York were playing an exhibition game in Jacksonville, Florida, when a pitch from Brooklyn pitcher Jeff Pfeffer struck Chick Fewster, the Yankees' second baseman, in the right temple, causing him to fall unconscious at home plate. After he was treated, a doctor accompanied him north to Johns Hopkins Hospital in Baltimore. The X-rays revealed a skull fracture with hemorrhaging and a blood clots. A two-hour operation removed the clots and a small piece of his skull. Afterwards Fewster was unable to speak for several days and did not return to the lineup until early July. Ray's teammates hoped for more positive results than that, but were somewhat reassured knowing that Fewster, after what he suffered, did eventually rejoin his team.

That evening the results came back showing a complicated skull fracture with hemorrhaging and at least several blood clots. Ray's blood pressure dropped to a dangerous low of near 50. In all probability, it was Tris Speaker and Cleveland's traveling secretary, Walter McNicholls, who huddled with the surgeons and gave permission to go ahead with the life-and-death operation. To attempt a telephone call to Ray's parents (Katy was on the train) for confirmation meant precious minutes wasted. Most of the tired ballplayers left for the team hotel, hoping to catch a few hours' sleep before Tuesday's game.

In the operating room at approximately 12:30 a.m. Tuesday morning, a team of surgeons cut into Ray's head to find a small piece of bone separated from the skull and pressing on the brain. They carefully removed it before moving on to address the blood clots and hemorrhaging. The surgeons noted ruptures on the right side of the skull as well as major damage to Ray's sinus cavity. All the skills and surgical techniques available in 1920 were used in the attempt to save the patient. But it was a catastrophic injury, the kind that did not fare well in an operating room or elsewhere. After an hour's work the doctors closed the incision and Ray was moved to a recovery room.

Within a short time his blood pressure rose to 90, giving everyone a small degree of hope. Speaker would not leave the hospital, refusing to sleep until Ray's condition had been stabilized or the alternative. This was his best friend in the world, a teammate of five years, a hunting and fishing partner. For the next hour or so he and the doctors waited for any significant developments.

In the early Tuesday morning hours Ray began to fail. His vital signs weakened; his pulse dropped precariously low again. The doctors had used up all their treatment options and could do no more to help him. The grave situation turned into a solemn death watch with Speaker and the physicians observing in vain. A few moments before 5:00 a.m., Ray breathed his last. He was now the only ballplayer in major league baseball history to perish from a pitched ball.

Because of the time of death, the Tuesday morning newspapers carried no information of Ray's passing. The afternoon and evening editions would break the story with extensive text along with quotes from various sources. When Katy and Jane stepped off the train around 10:30 a.m. at Grand Central Station, a silent delegation of Cleveland ballplayers and American League officials was waiting for them. The women were quickly escorted to Speaker's hotel room to be delivered the shocking news. Katy did not quite know for certain until she saw the woeful expression on the face of Ray's best pal.

The scene in the hotel room had to be one of the most sorrowful experiences a human being could be subjected to. Depending on the news reports, Katy either fainted or stood in disbelief at the horrible news. Her seemingly perfect world disintegrated in less than a blink of an eye. Her plans for Ray, the love of her life, the baby, the new house, grand vacations home and abroad, were now crushed forever. All that remained was to wait for the body to be released to her, then board the train for the unfathomable trip back to Cleveland. Mr. and Mrs. Daly received an updated telegram and hastily made plans to take a train to Utica, New York, to meet Katy and Jane for the balance of the trip home. Their lives would never be the same as they tried to support their bereaved daughter through her lengthy time of mourning.

Speaker sent a telegram to J. R. Johnson in Owensboro advising him of his nephew's death. Whether it was fortunate or ill-fated, Margaret Chapman, Ray's younger sister, was with Johnson for a visit. Her aunt and uncle put her on a train for Herrin to meet her parents for the wretched trip to Cleveland. Their last visit with Ray had been some six months earlier, just before the start of spring training and the extended Chapman honeymoon.

Ray's body was moved to a funeral parlor on Amsterdam Avenue to wait there for Wednesday's removal to the train station. Everyone urged Katy not to see Ray until the body reached the Daly home in Cleveland. His face likely had a great deal of swelling due to the head fracture and multiple bruises near his left eye. She agreed to wait at least until the Cleveland mortuary could prepare Ray for the funeral.

Many New Yorkers made the trip to Amsterdam Avenue to pay their respects to the fallen shortstop. The Yankees front office mercifully called off Tuesday's game, allowing the players a little time to gather their thoughts before playing on Wednesday. Speaker had already decided to accompany the body to Cleveland, selecting Joe Wood, another close friend of Ray, to make the trip with him, Katy, and Jane.

While arrangements were being made, Speaker paused to give a statement to the *Cleveland News*. The grieving manager told the paper, "Ray Chapman was the best friend I have ever had and as such I will mourn and miss him as much as on the baseball diamond. I doubt if he had an enemy even among his opponents and his untimely death will cast a gloom over ball players in general as well as each individual Cleveland player in particular."

Throughout the day Tuesday, the Cleveland players drifted in and out of the Ansonia Hotel lobby as if shell-shocked. When the news came Steve O'Neill went into an absolute rage, declaring he was going to hunt Mays down and rip him into small pieces. His teammates were forced to keep him in his hotel room with the door locked from the outside.

Jack Graney told the newspapermen that he doubted he and the others could pull themselves together and continue to play ball. But no matter how grim they felt, they had no option but to play out the schedule. In 1920 there were no grief counselors, and few places to go for any kind of therapy session. The players would have to try putting their thoughts for Ray aside while continuing the fight for the pennant.

Wednesday's news headlines across the country were all about the tragic death of Ray Chapman. Full pages were devoted to the incident as well as commentary with personal reflections from friends and ballplayers. One of the most tender was delivered by Larry Lajoie, who had played alongside Ray for several seasons. Larry told the *Cleveland News,* "He was a wonderful kid when he broke in. He was an apt pupil and I never saw a youngster more ambitious to learn and get ahead. I was glad of the chance to have such a wonderful character as Chappie as my running mate." Lajoie added that he would offer his services to Speaker for no pay, but too many years had gone by for him to don a uniform again.

Ed Bang, the well-respected sports editor for the *News,* had kept a strong relationship with Ray for the last eight years. The paper's story did not have a byline to it, but surely Bang was the author. "Chappie stood like a million dollars with the newspaper boys [writers] all over the American League circuit. There was a reason and a good one of course. He said to this writer several years ago, I used to think it wasn't right for the newspaper boys to criticize the ball players the way they do at times, but I realized that I was wrong and that they are paid for writing criticisms of the game and the players as they see things and not as we think they should see them."

Probably the most heart-rending sentiment came from Fred Lieb. He sent a check to Ed Bang to buy a floral arrangement for Katy, adding the words "In all my experience as a newspaper reporter, I have never wrote of a thing that touched me deeper than the unfortunate end of a lovable young chap." Lieb succinctly expressed sentiments that all the mourners could relate to.

On Wednesday morning at 10:00 a.m., the New York Central train carrying Ray's coffin eased into Cleveland's Union Station. A large troupe of Clevelanders stood by, quietly watching the casket being gently removed from the train. The body was taken to the undertakers, Hogan and Company, in the downtown area to be prepared for the Friday funeral.

Katy and Jane left the group for the Daly home to isolate themselves from the throng of people wishing to offer condolences. Katy had not been able to escape the crowds of sympathetic people since Tuesday morning. At home she grieved privately with her immediate family and tried to compose herself somehow for the services less than two days away. Huge flower arrangements along with cards arrived by the hour at the Euclid Avenue house, sincere gestures to a widow and family trying to cope with the tremendous sorrow.

A ballgame did take place at the Polo Grounds, but both team's players and New York fans stayed relatively quiet through most of the afternoon. The twenty-four flags at the top of the grandstand were lowered to half-mast in tribute to Ray. Harry Lunte started at shortstop, while Charlie Jamieson replaced Speaker in center field. The Indians were actually winning 3–2 going into the bottom of the ninth, but the Yankees plated two runs to take the game, 4–3.

Carl Mays was not in uniform for the Wednesday contest. Of all the sympathy expressed the day before, the pitcher received little from the players and writers. Though Mays was an excellent starting pitcher, a dominant twenty-game winner in 1917 and 1918, he still had an unshakable reputation as a man who had no qualms about throwing inside. In the process he had hit more than a few batters square in the head.

In April of 1917, pitching for Boston, Mays drew the ire of many when he hit A's outfielder Frank Thatcher above the ear, knocking him cold. After the incident the Philadelphia sportswriter Robert Maxwell wrote tongue-in-cheek that Thatcher now batted with one foot in the batter's box and the other in the grandstand. According to Maxwell, a short time later Mays threw twice at George Burns's head, then missed with the third pitch, only striking Burns in the ribs. It was meant to be humorous, but the point was made.

Mays could be the center of controversy even when he was not pitching. Before his time with the Yankees, the Red Sox were in Philadelphia playing a Memorial Day doubleheader. Game two went to extra innings, and the A's rallied in the bottom of the tenth. Several of their fans, sitting behind the visitor's dugout, began to pound on the iron railings directly behind the bench. Without warning, Mays came out of the dugout and fired a ball point blank at the noisemakers. It narrowly missed an innocent woman but struck one of the offenders on the top of the head, smashing his newly worn straw hat. The gentleman, a government employee, sought out a policeman to demand an arrest for assault and battery. Connie Mack talked the fan out of it and into going to the station later and asking for an arrest warrant. Mays was thus able to leave Philadelphia before the warrant was obtained and served. Apparently, over time, the injured party lost interest, allowing any charges against the pitcher to disappear. New straw hats were relatively inexpensive, less than court costs and hiring an attorney.

In July of 1919 Mays abruptly quit the Red Sox, refusing to play until traded. Most American League teams declined to deal for him, but the Yankees did, getting more than a few successful seasons from the controversial pitcher. The day Ray died from his injury, two teams, the Red Sox and Tigers, drew up petitions demanding Mays be thrown out of organized baseball. Like everyone in baseball, both teams had great sympathy for Ray, but Ty Cobb and the Detroit men had had no love for the pitcher after a beanball incident with Ty several years earlier, and the Red Sox disliked their former teammate for the way he left in 1919.

The St. Louis players did not go that far but expressed their bitterness toward Mays stemming from a beanball episode involving George Sisler. It was apparently the only time the premier hitter challenged an opposing player to fight on the field. One St. Louis writer believed that if the Browns had received a telegram about Ray's death but no mention of the pitcher responsible, to a man they would have guessed Mays. The petitions and the thought of other clubs joining in only brought more unwanted publicity to major league baseball.

Ross Tenney, sportswriter for the *Cleveland Press*, put his views on the front page. His article, titled "Ban the Bean Ball," called for an end to any deliberate inside pitching. Tenney wrote, "There is no charge that pitcher Carl Mays intentionally hit Ray Chapman. Players exonerated him. But Chappie is dead. Whether the ball was thrown intentionally or unintentionally, the result is the same. And there is the feeling that Chappie would be alive and at short today if there had been a heavy penalty against throwing of the kind of ball that hit him."

Tenney wanted the major leagues to institute a penalty of two bases for the batter and two for any baserunners for an intentionally thrown inside pitch. He believed that would stop any beanballs, especially in a tight game. He cited two minor league players killed by pitched balls and wrote about the retired player-manager of the Cubs and Yankees, Frank Chance, who had been hit several times in the head, eventually needing surgery. The *Cleveland News* published a three-column letter from a fan imploring Mays to retire from pitching and try to reinvent himself as an outfielder or infielder. The fan believed his pitching style was too difficult for batters to handle and could cause another incident like the one that happened to Ray.

The controversy surrounding Mays continued throughout his career and beyond. In early April of 1922, after a morning round of golf, he took the hill for an exhibition game against Brooklyn. The Dodgers hitters teed off on him in the early going. Manager Huggins called time, visibly angry at his start-er's performance so close to the regular season. The two ex-changed words before Mays took the ball and hurled it over the grandstand. Huggins was incensed, taking his pitcher out of the game and later fining him a hefty $200 for "Insubordination and Rowdiness." Mays told the newspapers he would not pay the fine and that he would rather retire from baseball. Appar-ently he backed down, as he played for the Yankees through the 1923 season. He finished his career in Cincinnati, then spent most of his life trying to restore his reputation.

Before the funeral, Tris Speaker apparently met with the Yankees owners and agreed to issue a statement designed to calm the waters. The New York evening papers carried the statement from Tris: "On the part of two or three of our players there is some bitterness toward Mays, but I am going to do all I can to suppress it and any bitterness that might arise. For the good of baseball, for the good of the players themselves, and especially out of regard for the poor fellow that's dead, it is our duty to do that." He did not indicate who the bitter players were, but a betting man would say Jack Graney, Steve O'Neill, and likely Joe Wood. The baseball owners were aghast that some of their players were speaking out; Athletics owner Connie Mack thought it was up to him to speak on behalf of the bosses, saying, "I for one believe Chapman's death was an accident pure and simple. The unfortunate part of it all is that it happened to be Mays who pitched the ball that hit Chapman. I admit there was a time when we thought he used the bean ball, but not this year." Apparently that was Mack's way of supporting Mays, who did not need any half-baked testimony on his behalf. American League President Ban Johnson handled it the right way, deflecting all talk while making certain the remaining owners kept their players in check. The Red Sox and Tiger petitions went nowhere.

Mays would argue that the ball was scuffed, damp, and dirty and should have been tossed out by the home plate umpire. This claim has a ring of truth to it, as umpires in those days would bring in new balls only when absolutely necessary. The pitcher further mentioned he had thought about paying a visit to Katy Chapman to express his sympathy, but Colonel Huston advised him to stay away. Mays was in a dreadful situation, unable to garner much support anywhere. Even though Speaker publicly exonerated him, he would always be the guy who killed Ray Chapman with a pitched ball. If any other hurler had been the one to throw the deadly pitch, chances are they would not have come under nearly as much scrutiny in the press or the world of public opinion as Carl Mays endured.

On Thursday, Martin Daly announced that the funeral would be held at St. Philomena, officiated by Father Smith. Burial plans were incomplete due to an issue between the two families. Ray may have talked about converting to Catholicism, but he never took the steps to make it a reality. Newspapers reported Daly sent a priest to Ray's bedside to give prayer at the end, while stories persisted that if the patient awoke the priest would have offered last rites and a conversion to Catholicism.

This did not occur, meaning Ray's final resting place could not be in the Daly plot at Calvary Cemetery. The Chapmans and probably Speaker, whom the family trusted, all had input into where to bury the deceased. After discussion with Martin Daly, the place of burial decided on was Lake View Cemetery, one of the Midwest's finest cemeteries. The invoice for the large plot had Katy's name on it.

The 285 acres of burial grounds stand on rolling hills overlooking downtown Cleveland. With many large trees along with colorful flowers throughout, it's a picturesque setting with memorials for national figures, including President James A. Garfield, Jeptha Wade (of Western Union Telegraph), and, some years after Ray's death, one of the country's wealthiest men, industrialist John D. Rockefeller.

Though it was an ideal place for a gravesite, Katy would unlikely be able to join her husband there. The Daly family plot at Calvary was purchased by Daly for himself, his wife, and their five children. She would come under the family rule to take her place at Calvary, even if she made her wishes known to be buried at Lakeview with Ray. On the plus side, Lake View Cemetery stood only blocks from the Daly home, close enough for Katy to visit and take their child whenever she needed to. The unhappy fact remained, however, that husband and wife were destined to be separated for eternity.

Later on Thursday, Martin Daly realized that several thousand people would be converging on St. Philomena to attend services. The church could not accommodate such a large contingent, pressing Daly to obtain permission from the highest-ranking clergy to transfer the venue to St. John's Cathedral, one of the largest and most venerable churches in northeast Ohio. St. John's officially opened in 1852 on the corner of Erie Street (now East Ninth) in downtown Cleveland and is an architectural wonder, magnificent in scope and featuring sandstone trim along with one-of-a-kind large art glass windows brought in 1902 from Munich, Germany. The cathedral was and continues to be the home of the Catholic Diocese of Cleveland. Despite less than a day to plan the services, it promised to be an extravagant funeral, one to be remembered for many years.

11
SAYING GOODBYE

At precisely 8:35 a.m. on Friday, the New York Central train carrying the Cleveland club rolled into Union Station. The distraught players had only about an hour to get themselves in proper attire for the funeral. Five autos were waiting at the Daly home to take them to St. John's Cathedral as part of the funeral procession west down Euclid Avenue to Ninth Street.

By 9:00 a.m. mourners began to line up on the steps and sidewalks of the chapel. The sanctuary was reserved for family and friends of Ray along with the priests from several churches. Once all the parties were seated, a limited number of people would be granted entrance. Some folks brought stepladders to prop up outside the church windows to take a glance at the proceedings. Many others headed for any place close to the entrance steps, hoping to at least see the funeral party as they entered.

Packed into the large crowd were hundreds of little boys who idolized Ray. They had many times greeted him outside of League Park before games, cheering him on with cries of "Hello Chappie" and "A home run today!" Ray always waved and smiled at the boys, promising to bring home a win. Now they gathered on the church steps or across the street, heads bowed in silence, caps in hand, waiting for the long procession to arrive.

Police officers on foot and horseback struggled to keep the avenues open around St. John's, but traffic was snarled with hundreds of cars trying to park in the vicinity of the cathedral. The multitude reached an estimated 5,000 people attempting to reach the church in hopes of finding space to watch from the outside. The crowd reportedly either topped or came close to a record number for a Cleveland funeral.

Near 10:00 the procession slowly arrived at East Ninth Street, led by a white hearse bearing Ray's coffin. The people assembled on the church steps had to squeeze together to make a narrow path for the coffin and mourners to be brought up the steps. The top of the casket had a sizable blanket of pink roses, donated by citizens of Cleveland from all parts of the community. All told, over 2,000 roses were bought at a dime apiece to honor Ray. Civic leaders proposed that the money left over, roughly $1,700, be set aside to build a bronze memorial for Ray, to be mounted inside the entrance to League Park. The committee promised to speak with Katy about the makeup of the plaque and present her and Ray's mother with duplicates.

As the procession climbed the stairs, the powerful bells of St. John's tolled, creating an air of solemnity that captured the attention of all present. Among the pallbearers were Steve O'Neill, Joe Wood, Tom Raftery, who had played briefly for Cleveland and was a longtime friend of Ray, plus the two oldest Daly brothers, Walter and Martin Jr. Ray's mother requested that one of her son's best friends from Owensboro be brought up to help carry the coffin, and Martin Daly quickly obliged. It was one of the few requests made by Ray's family. Just behind the sober pallbearers, walking painstakingly slowly, was a bro-kenhearted Katy, dressed in deep black and leaning heavily on her father's arm for support. As she made her way by the crowd, men and women burst into tears at the sight of the devastated young widow.

Following closely, the four Chapmans along with the rest of the Dalys made their way to the reserved pews inside the church. Completing the procession were James Dunn and American League president Ban Johnson, and trailing behind them the stunned members of the Cleveland baseball club walking in pairs. If there could be any lighthearted moment, it happened when the casket reached the doors. At that instant a group of the young boys made a quick sprint for the entrance. The police standing by gave a less than spirited effort to hold them back. They were "Chappie's boys," and all knew Ray would have wanted them inside.

The Mass commenced at 10:15 with a church choir, assembled earlier at St. Philomena. Aware the Chapmans were not Catholic, the singers included two Protestant hymns in their selections, including "Lead, Kindly Light." The service continued until close to 11:00 a.m. Dr. William Scullen, chancellor of the Catholic Diocese of Cleveland, delivered the sermon. Dr. Scullen, a noted baseball and football fan, served as one of the leading voices in the religious affairs of Cleveland and was always a sought-after speaker for civic events and church dedications. He had aided the diocese since 1915.

Dr. Scullen's words were eloquent and compelling, evoking images of Ray as a warm, compassionate man who loved his family and friends. "To the small boy, the grown man, the aged, he was ever the same and to those whose privilege it was to know him he was the friend that and the soul ever serene, the friend that understands, the friend that sympathizes, the friend that knows our weaknesses but still loves us. This was a man, the idol of a city, the idol of other cities wherein he displayed his prowess as an athlete but above all greatness and kindness as a man."

Dr. Scullen, with all of the congregation leaning on every word, ended his sermon with a message to the Cleveland ball club: "May his team-mates carry on the same spirit—play clean, fair, honest baseball, striving to win and bring to him the tribute that he sought. He was born, he has lived, he is no more, but his spirit still lives. May the soul of the gently kindly youth whom Heaven knows, rest in peace." After a moment of silence, the choir sang, followed by the pallbearers rising and carrying Ray's casket for the ride east of downtown to Lake View Cemetery. Once again the police had difficulty in clearing Euclid Avenue, this time to allow the hearse and family to depart the area.

At the cemetery a brief service was conducted, followed by placing the coffin in a vault for burial at a later date. A thousand or two bright pink roses were strewn about the grounds in a final tribute to the fallen hero, and a huge number of floral arrangements were placed in front of the vault, including a large baseball and a ballfield, complete with an outfield and a pitcher's mound with four bases. People who did not personally know Ray went to great expense to contribute something in his memory.

The newly formed Ray Chapman Memorial Committee finalized plans to publish a commemorative leather-bound edition of Dr. Scullen's sermon. Once completed, copies would be distributed to the Chapmans, Dalys, all Ray's teammates, as well as selected friends. The volume would also include a colorized image of the memorial plaque placed before the printed sermon.

The extraordinary funeral had ended; it was time for the Chapman and Daly families to begin the long, almost impossible healing process over the loss of a devoted son, husband, and son-in-law. For Ray's mom the process became unbearable. She found it difficult to leave her bedroom, even sending Margaret away for several months to live with her sister in Owensboro. Today, relatives say that Mrs. Chapman never fully recovered from Ray's untimely death, although she lived many decades beyond.

For the Cleveland Indians, there was no time to reconcile their thoughts. A doubleheader with Boston awaited on Saturday along with a road trip lasting through the first days of September. They departed Cleveland without their player-manager, who could not summon the strength to play baseball for the time being. He would join his teammates five days later, but the skid that had begun with the first Yankees series continued throughout August as the Indians fell out of first place. Fortunately, the White Sox and Yankees failed to take advantage. The White Sox at one point lost seven in a row, and the Yankees were unable to put together any kind of winning streak, allowing Cleveland to stay on their heels.

Near the finish of the trying road trip, the Indians were in Washington taking infield practice. A cameraman approached Speaker asking for permission to shoot a group photo. Speaker emphatically told the gentleman his team would not do it. As he explained to reporters, "I wouldn't ask the boys to pose before the start of a game. We had a picture taken at the Polo Grounds just prior to the contest in which Chappie met his end. Some of the boys regard it as an ill omen and I know they would not consent to lining up now. Back home during morning practice they probably would not balk, but nothing doing now." Despite the temporary ban, there are a number of team photos, post-Ray, of the 1920 ball club circulating. One has a head shot of Ray added to the image, placed in a star above his teammates.

On September 3 the Indians returned to League Park to start a long homestand that would last most of the month. The first game, against Detroit, was designated Ray Chapman Day and featured a service half an hour before play began. The Naval Reserves took part, with a bugler playing "Taps" along with the raising of Old Glory to half-mast. A combined church choir of one hundred voices sang "Lead, Kindly Light" accompanied by a full orchestra. Thousands of memorial programs were handed out to the fans, including the text of Dr. Scullen's sermon with biographical information about Ray.

Martin Daly, who attended the game alone, bought several thousand copies from the printer to distribute to his workers at the East Ohio Gas Company. Ban Johnson purchased 2,000 more, for all the teams in the American League and anyone connected to baseball. The scorecard for the afternoon had a black border around the cover.

The *Cleveland News* filled its pages with stories about the memorial service and the game itself. The editors bemoaned the loss of Ray, philosophizing on what it meant for the ball club. An article stated, "Friday was the Indians first appearance at League Park since Ray Chapman met an untimely death by being hit in the head with a pitched ball thrown by Carl Mays at the Polo Grounds, New York, August 16. Somehow or other it didn't seem right without Chappie cavorting around the short field in practice and during the game. The old 'Chatter Box' was not there and there was an aching void in the hearts of hundreds of the 18,000 odd fans who turned out to pay tribute to his memory."

Before the ballgame, Speaker had some upbeat words for the writers. "I feel certain that we are going to win the pennant despite the irreparable loss we sustained in the sudden taking off of Ray Chapman." They were brave thoughts from the player-manager, who was still trying to find his composure while leading his team forward.

In spite of the damper on the afternoon, a well-played game saw Cleveland lose again by a score of 1–0. Despite the loss, those 18,000-odd fans managed to cheer mightily for the players from the onset. They applauded during fielding and batting practice, then stood, shouting encouragement, as each player came to bat throughout the game. Harry Lunte, the fill-in shortstop, received a thunderous ovation. When Elmer Smith smashed a triple, several hundred straw hats from the crowd were hurled onto the field in celebration. Moments later, in a show of solidarity, when Smith was easily thrown out at home trying to score on Larry Gardner's short fly to right field, no boos were heard from the crowd.

The fans' attitude, after the disappointing road trip, showed compassion for the stressful times the players were going through. The rooters knew how difficult it was to lose a dear friend, one loved by all. James Lanyon, the sports editor for the *Plain Dealer*, was moved to write a column about what he witnessed. "The Cleveland Indians played their first home game for a long time yesterday and lost," he said. "But they were given as warm a welcome as any victorious army ever was given." Lanyon mentioned the rousing applause for Tigers shortstop Donie Bush, who had said he would play shortstop for Cleveland if the American League would allow it. He wrote about the huge ovation for Bill Wamby, when earlier in the season the fans often yelled for Joe Wood or George Burns to hit for him. The fans, he concluded, "were decent in every respect. They were fans with soul."

The massive fan support helped the psyche of the Cleveland ballplayers, in search of something to lift their spirits since Ray's death, and went a long way to shaking them out of their lethargy. They started winning again and did not stop, closing out September with a record of 20–6 for the month.

With the fans' help, as well as the September 8 arrival of rookie shortstop Joe Sewell, the Indians played championship baseball. Fresh from the New Orleans Pelicans, Sewell gave the team a spark, more so with his bat than his fielding. He had some problems throwing accurately to first but hit as well as or better than Ray, with a batting average of .329 over the last three weeks of the season.

Sewell was a mere twenty years old when he joined the Indians. He would later talk about being a boy from a small town in Alabama, not quite ready to live in a large city like Cleveland. He left home with just one cotton suit, fine for southern living but hardly enough for autumn in the Midwest. On the train north to Cleveland, the conductor noticed this and arranged for Sewell to see a tailor in Cincinnati, one of the stops on the way. Working quickly, the tailor put together a heavy wool suit, just right for uncertain fall weather off Lake Erie.

At the time few in baseball could be certain how a young man such as Sewell could handle the job in such dire circumstances. It was one thing to fill in for an injured player, but another to try and replace an idol who had recently passed away. But he accomplished it, proving to be a more than ample replacement and going on to become one of Cleveland's greatest shortstops along with Ray.

With Sewell now in the lineup and Walter "Duster" Mails, fresh from the Pacific Coast League, added to the pitching staff, Cleveland would not be denied, outdistancing the White Sox and Yankees. The pennant was theirs, with the World Series to come versus the Brooklyn Robins. The ballplayers and the city had come a remarkably long way since August 17, overcoming tremendous adversity to claim the American League championship. Only one issue remained to be solved: the eligibility of Joe Sewell. The major league rules stated that having joined the Indians in late August, he was ineligible for the postseason roster. However, due to the extenuating circumstances, a waiver was granted allowing Sewell to play in the series.

The World Series in 1920 was best of nine games, requiring teams to win five games instead of the usual four. The first three would be played in Brooklyn, the next four in Cleveland, and the last two in Brooklyn if necessary. The Indians played brilliantly, salvaging one game in Brooklyn and taking four straight at home to capture their first world championship. Those who witnessed the four games saw fabulous pitching from Stan Coveleski, Jim Bagby, and Walter Mails. The famous Wamby triple play happened in game five along with Elmer Smith's grand slam plus a three-run homer from pitcher Bagby, all firsts in World Series play.

The Cleveland players voted to send a full share of the winner's money to Katy. It was a symbolic gesture since she had more money than many of the players combined, but a thoughtful one nonetheless. A short time later she received an additional $5,000 payment from the ball club as an insurance settlement. Workman's compensation had been law in Cleveland for several years, but the Indians carried insurance through a private company. Again, Katy did not need the money, but the club's willingness to pay a widow still trying to make sense of her husband's death was commendable.

Katy moved out of the Superior Avenue rental home back to her parents' place for the immediate future. The lovely new home on Alvason went vacant; Katy never spent a single night there. In October the Dalys put the house up for sale, to be quickly purchased by Cleveland amateur baseball mogul Max Rosenblum. The owner of a prominent downtown clothing store, he was a good friend of the family along with the Cleveland ballplayers. He was also one of the members of the committee to design and build the bronze plaque for Ray. Rosenblum wanted to make the real estate transaction as trouble-free as possible for Katy. The papers reported the sale price to be $40,000, in today's money the equivalent of $592,000.

Though Ray was gone, the Chapman and Daly families maintained some communication, especially with a grandchild soon to be involved. Margaret Chapman would occasionally visit the Dalys in Cleveland. During one trip the hosts tried to talk Margaret into staying with them to enroll in a Cleveland-area college. It was a heartfelt gesture, but she preferred to be in Herrin with her lifelong friends.

Now that the Indians were world champs, Ray's poignant story began to be overshadowed by daily events, thoughts about the 1921 spring training, and the pursuit of another pennant. Time simply marches on, leaving behind memories of loved ones and other worthy occurrences to gradually find their way into the background.

However, there still were occasions when Ray's name became national news again. On February 27, 1921, Katy gave birth to a seven-pound little girl she named Rae Marie. The story made page 1 of the *Cleveland News,* with a photo of the new mother and article that said, "A living monument to perpetuate the memory of Ray Chapman came into being at St. Ann's Maternity Hospital when on Sunday afternoon a baby girl was born to Mrs. Kathleen Chapman." The story was syndicated to newspapers in most major cities across the country.

It was evident Katy wanted to cling to memories of her late husband, hence the constant reminder of him in her newborn daughter's first name. Rae, like her mom, would seemingly have a life of privilege ahead of her, orchestrated by the Dalys. The only disadvantage was a significant one: she would not have the opportunity to know her wonderful late father.

Before the opening of the regular season, students at Bowdoin College in Maine announced plans for a Ray Chapman memorial, in the form of a silver trophy. Even though Ray never attended Bowdoin or had any affiliation with it, the students intended to annually award the trophy, "the Ray Chapman Cup," to the American League shortstop who meant the most to his ball club. An extraordinary gesture from college students who had never come in contact with the late ballplayer.

The major league season kicked off in April with high expectations for the defending world champions. They played exceedingly well the first two months, posting a record of 29–14. On Saturday, May 7, a chauffeured automobile pulled up to League Park at Sixty-Sixth and Lexington and two attractive, well-dressed women in their twenties stepped out to the sidewalk. Gentlemen's heads swiveled, then spun around a second time as they realized the women were Katy Chapman and Jane McMahon. Mrs. Chapman had not been to a game at League Park since August 15 of last year. A buzz went through the crowd as the lifelong friends settled into their box seats to see Ray's former teammates in action. It may have been the one and only game she attended after her husband's death. Newspapers did not mention if she brought her baby daughter for the Cleveland players to meet.

Katy had recently filed with probate court to settle Ray's estate. He had failed to compose a will, not unusual for a recently married twenty-nine-year-old. His assets were slightly below $20,000, including a flashy 1920 Cole four-seater automobile valued at a high-priced $2,944. The car company operated out of Indianapolis, Indiana, specializing in high-performance V8 engines. Other assets listed were $300 in thrift stamps purchased during World War I. An alternative to buying war bonds, a stamp could be purchased for twenty-five cents. Sixteen of them netted you a war savings stamp that would be worth $5 at a certain point after the war ended. Ray likely picked them up when he had pocket change. He had a one-third interest in a warehouse and, curiously, twenty bottles of liquor, possibly left over after the wedding just before the start of Prohibition. Ray owned two hundred shares of stock in Pioneer Alloys, half preferred and the other half common with no value listed. His position at the company stayed with the family, being given to brother-in-law Walter Daly.

There were cash assets in various banks and bond holdings, which left the estate at the $20,000 figure. Other than the warehouse investment Ray had no real estate property; the spacious new home was strictly in his wife's name. It would take several years to fully settle the estate, but Katy, as administratrix, would be taking yearly payments of $6,000 until the money ran out. Ray, in his eight years and change in the major leagues along with several years in the minors, had accumulated a fair amount, the equivalent of close to $300,000 today. He still had ground to make up, but his salary at Pioneer Alloys in addition to his stock holdings had put him on a path to real wealth. Only a high inside fastball kept him from reaching the end of the rainbow.

On May 14 the Yankees invaded League Park to open up a four-game series. Carl Mays, who had not been to Cleveland since the August 1920 accident, was slated to pitch one of the games. In an effort to keep the Cleveland fans guessing, the New York management would not state which game. They did not want to take a chance on the locals filling the seats and harassing their pitcher or worse. Mays sat for the first two games, then started on Monday, traditionally a slow day at the box office. However, the fans were not fooled, guessing correctly Monday would be the day for Mays. By game time, there were over 12,000 in the seats. A large police presence circled the field just in case anyone in the grandstand tried to settle personally with the Yankee pitcher.

In the top of the first Bob Meusel blasted a three-run home run off Walter Mails to stake Mays to a lead. The submariner took the mound with little reaction from the assembled in the grandstand, beyond a smattering of applause from a small delegation of New Yorkers in town to see the series.

In the top of seventh inning the game was tied at 3, when Mays came to bat. Whether manager Speaker or catcher O'Neill gave the signal to Mails, the first pitch was a fastball rocketing toward the batter's head. Mays barely evaded the line of fire, and the fans let out a tremendous roar. After all this time a distinct measure of payback had been achieved. Nobody got hurt, nobody went to a hospital, but a clear message was sent by "Duster" Mails. The Yankees pitcher slowly rose to his feet, understanding the Cleveland contingent had not forgotten what happened to Ray on August 17, 1920. Baseball justice at its finest. Strangely, only the *Plain Dealer* reported what took place. The *News* and *Press* said nothing.

The next pitch was high and inside. A cautious Mays stuck out his bat in self-defense and lifted a weak pop fly to the infield. The Yankees scored again in the top of the ninth to win the game 6–3, taking three out of four from Cleveland. The 12,000 fans left the ballpark disappointed in the loss and the whole series but with a measure of satisfaction from the two beanballs served up by Mails.

There were more opportunities to honor Ray's memory, one being the one-year anniversary of his death. Martin Daly saw to it that a special Mass in Ray's name would be held at St. Philomena Church. The Mass took place on August 17 each year into the 1960s. In time it changed venues, being transferred to St. Dominic Church in Shaker Heights, where at least one of the Daly children was a member.

On the baseball side, Jim Dunn wanted to keep things low-key, but changed his mind and ordered several thousand roses to be distributed to fans attending the August 17, 1921, game. There were no advertisements in the newspapers announcing this, so attendance was only around the 6,000 mark.

Philadelphia brought their hitting shoes with them, scoring four runs in the top of the first inning. Charlie Jamieson led off the bottom half with a screaming line drive in the direction of first baseman Johnny Walker. The baseball took a sharp bounce on the concrete-like infield turf, then caromed off the right side of Walker's head. The force of it spun him around and he fell face first on the ground, unconscious. Fortunately, there was a doctor in the house in the person of Indians backup left fielder Joe Evans, who had recently been licensed to practice medicine. He attended to the first baseman until he regained consciousness some ten minutes later.

Two A's players helped Walker to the visitor's clubhouse, where Evans called for an ambulance. The two rode to Lakeside Hospital, where Dr. Castle was to take them back for immediate X-rays. The results were negative, no skull fracture, but a concussion that would hospitalize Walker for the balance of two weeks. He remained semiconscious and in great pain. The timing of Walker's injury was spine-chilling, to say the least. Everyone at League Park naturally thought of the fatal beaning exactly one year ago.

Dr. Evans sent word to the ballpark that Walker would recover, easing the minds of both teams. In the bottom of the fifth inning, Bill Wamby, leading off, took the first pitch from Rollie Naylor. Umpire Billy Evans called for time and the whole Indians team stepped out of the dugout and bowed their heads in silence for one minute in a final tribute to Ray. The fans all rose to do the same. Martin Daly stood in Jim Dunn's private box, watching the proceedings and likely thinking back to a year ago when the phone rang at the Euclid Avenue home with the dreadful news. Katy had declined to come to the ballpark, which turned out to be a providential decision. Had she seen another man take a blow to the head on the baseball field, it might have been too much to bear.

With a year gone by, Katy would try and put her life back together with a little girl to raise and the firm support of her parents, brothers, and sister. She did reappear in public to host a dance for a young men's club, but sightings of her were few and far between. In the winter of 1923 she suddenly married her cousin, Joseph Francis McMahon. The marriage took place in Los Angeles, where J.F., a major executive of Formax Oil, kept his residence. From the family, only Martin Daly and son Walter attended the wedding. The abruptness of the marriage along with the location, as far away from Cleveland, Ohio, as possible, raised several questions. Why would she leave everything behind to marry a cousin ten years older than she? How did the two of them see each other before the wedding, fall in love, and mutually agree to take up residence on the West Coast? The curious fact later emerged that Katy had bought and paid for the Los Angeles home along with the furnishings.

The Dalys might have had some involvement in attempting to get their daughter to move on with her life and the haunting memories of Ray behind. There were too many reminders of him in Cleveland through friends, acquaintances, and ballplayers who regularly came and went through town. To remove Katy from all of this and put her in the care of a forty-year-old trusted family member must have seemed like the proper thing to do. In 1923 single or widowed women with children were not usually expected to fend for themselves. Society decreed that women needed husbands to care for them and to keep them safe.

The McMahons celebrated their marriage with a honeymoon in Hawaii. Each winter afterwards Katy returned there, but mostly with her mother, Rae, or Jane McMahon, not J.F. Jane was a real trouper, taking the train all the way from Buffalo just to spend a few weeks with her dearest friend. It had to be a great comfort to Katy, but all was not well in southern California.

In October 1926 Katy gave birth to Joseph Francis McMahon Jr. in what should have been a joyous event. The happiness, if any, was short-lived as she began to see a doctor about her mental state. Though six years had passed, and despite a new family and life in sunny southern California, Katy's deep sense of loss over Ray's death still overwhelmed her.

Dr. James Johnston took over her personal care, sending her for periodic rests at a high-end L.A. County sanitarium. At the time there were few qualified people to give her any tangible benefit other than cold or warm baths and leisurely walks through the well-maintained hospital gardens. These treatments were believed to help the patient relax, calming their inner demons. Dr. Sigmund Freud invented psychoanalysis, but too little too late for a woman unable to cope with day-to-day living. There simply weren't the means for sufficient care of patients like Katy. For better or worse, Dr. Johnston, at his discretion, would send her back and forth between the facility and her well-appointed home in downtown Los Angeles.

A month before Joe was born, Katy had received news of the death of her father, Martin. While working at his desk at East Ohio he had suffered a massive heart attack and died moments later, at age sixty-six. For his daughter, still unable to come to grips with the memories of her late husband, this loss was the crowning blow to her fragile existence. The sanitarium stays became more frequent, with little improvement in her condition.

At the time, psychologists claimed that women's brains were inferior to men's. Women were believed to be emotional, with instinctive predispositions, while men were said to be non-expressive, keeping things in check, a superior trait. For Katy, there was nothing to prevent her from doing something impulsive, like attempting suicide.

The period when someone leaves supervised care to resume life at home can be dangerous if the person is not watched closely. On April 21, 1928, Katy left the Los Angeles sanitarium under the premise of arranging for the annual trip to Hawaii. She had been at home only a short time when she picked up a bottle of poison and drank the contents down. Mrs. Daly was at the house but could not have been aware what her thirty-four-year-old daughter had in mind to do. The initial reports out of Los Angeles said Katy had mistaken the poison for the medicine she had been prescribed. But this seems unlikely considering that liquid medication is usually taken with a spoon rather than drunk straight from the bottle.

The L.A. County coroner conducted an immediate autopsy and determined the cause of death as suicide. Dr. Johnston refused to add any information to the death certificate but did send a telegram to the Reverend Joseph Smith in Cleveland, reading, "Was in ill health for six months. Was recently released from psychiatric hospital. As witness of the fact can state her suicide was unpremeditated and done on impulse while mentally deranged." Disturbing words from the attending doctor, but apparently Katy, in the grip of profound despair, resolved to end her life. At that moment the means were there, and she acted.

Her body was sent home to Cleveland, where funeral services were conducted once again by Father Smith, who had married Ray and Katy in 1919. Being called on to preside over their funerals too, just eight years apart, was a sad irony. Despite the Catholic Church's firm stance against suicide, the burial occurred at Calvary Cemetery in the Daly family plot. There is a simple marker there for Kathleen McMahon, with no mention of Raymond Chapman.

Katy, just like her late first husband, did not prepare a will. Probate records showed her with assets near $85,000, or in today's money $1.4 million, which included the $25,000 house on South Irving Boulevard and a snappy Marmon Speedster automobile. Manufactured in Indianapolis, these were highly sought-after cars the average person could not afford. Though struggling with her mental health, Katy still carried the debutante in her, tooling around Los Angeles in an eye-catching sports car.

The estate was divided in thirds, with husband J.R., daughter Rae, and son Joseph Jr. receiving the balance of the assets.

In settling the estate, J.F. sold the home and all the furnishings, along with the auto. He moved on with his life, buying a new house while sending both children back to Cleveland to be raised there. Whatever he thought about Katy and their brief marriage has been lost, but the five years were surely fraught with pain and sorrow for both.

In less than a decade Ray and Katy were reduced to bittersweet memories for those who knew them. Two lives of infinite potential were abruptly cut short, leaving a young daughter behind to be reared without parents. Even with the best care available, almost a year to the day after her mother died, Rae Marie shockingly passed away in Cleveland from complications due to meningitis. She had lived only eight short years. It was another inexplicable tragedy that followed the Chapman and Daly families. The remaining members survived by keeping the memories to themselves, rarely speaking about their lost ones in public. Today, surviving members of the Daly family have little knowledge of Ray and Katy other than a few anecdotes.

The passing of Rae revealed an eight-year-old with the wealth of a successful adult. Through her late parents, stepfather, and grandparents, she had accumulated stocks and bonds in her name worth upwards of $35,000. Her probate records showed 202 shares of Standard Oil, 135 shares of F. B. Stearns (a longtime Cleveland automobile manufacturer), and 60 shares of Formax Oil, among others. Rae already had the financials necessary for a promising life. Her possessions were distributed to her younger half brother, Joseph Jr.

In August of 1920 Ray Chapman was still a young man, a prime example of someone living and successfully pursuing the elusive American dream. Raised in rural, small-town America, he overcame all obstacles in his path to reap the benefits of what society had to offer. He was not just an elite baseball player but a fledging business executive with a lovely wife and friends at every turn, along with a child on the way to love and care for, and about to move into a new home in an exclusive section of Cleveland. In mid-August the Indians were firmly in the pennant race, something Ray had been waiting for since his promotion to Cleveland in 1912. Everything he had ever wanted in baseball and outside of it was well within his reach when the ball club arrived in New York on Monday, August 16. At moments like these Ray Chapman thrived. He was there in the fight, doing his utmost to win, when an errant fastball, a little too high, too inside, ended his life.

Today one can travel to Lake View Cemetery any day of the week and visit Ray's large gravesite, located at the top of a small hill. Usually there are baseballs, hats, gloves, all types of memorabilia left by visitors to demonstrate what he meant to Cleveland. A short walk away is the grave of Charles Pinkney Jr., a twenty-two-year-old minor league second baseman killed in 1910 by a pitched ball in Dayton, Ohio. The circumstances were similar: gray skies and limited visibility. Pinkney's father was at the ballgame, rushing from the stands and carrying his boy to the clubhouse. His skull fractured, he only had hours to live. Ten years later it happened again, a gifted young man struck down well before his time. Though more than a century has passed, he is not lost to history. To this day, Raymond Johnson Chapman remains a shining star in Cleveland baseball lore and beyond.

Epilogue

Ray Chapman's major league career lasted seven full seasons and parts of two others. His 1912 debut campaign was slightly more than a month, while his last season ended a month and a half early. At that juncture in the schedule he had recorded a batting average of .303, with 132 hits and 97 runs scored in 111 games. He had his usual number of sacrifices with 41. Projecting his stats over an entire season, he likely would have had 175–180 hits and 125–130 runs scored. At the time of his death he ranked third in scoring, trailing only Babe Ruth and Tris Speaker. Ray was experiencing his finest season to date, just entering his prime years as a ballplayer.

What would he have accomplished had he hit the dirt, avoiding the deadly fastball? Probably another few seasons of batting .300 while scoring 100 or more runs each year and making spectacular plays at shortstop. Though Joe Sewell played admirably at the position, Ray's presence might have brought a second consecutive pennant to Cleveland. He was the catalyst of the ball club, the player who made things happen on a constant basis. His nonstop enthusiasm and "ginger" rubbed off on his teammates, producing a winning environment game after game.

In spite of his relatively short career, Ray is among the leaders in several categories in Cleveland's all-time list. His 238 steals place him fifth and his 671 runs scored have him in eighteenth place. Had he played just one more season, he would likely have positioned himself in top-ten territory. A full career might have put him in consideration for baseball's Hall of Fame. Unfortunately, no film of Ray in action exists, nor are there many detailed testimonials from his teammates, other than what was said at the time of his death. However, based on the newspaper reporting of the 1910s through 1920, his ability at shortstop was on another level compared to his peers.

As the years rolled by, Ray's name would appear in print, usually in "On This Date in Baseball" columns or an occasional letter to the sports editor on the circumstances of his death. In 1924 Honus Wagner was asked to list his all-time American League team from the beginnings in 1901 through 1923. Though he had only played in the National League, Wagner named Ray to the team along with the Ruths, Cobbs, and Speakers, saying, "Chapman had no fear at all, he was extremely aggressive and very confident. All ball players loved Ray." Wagner believed the Cleveland shortstop would have been one of the all-time greats had he lived, adding that there was no play Ray could not make. "He was one of those boys who played baseball as if he loved it better than anything else on Earth."

Two years later, when pitcher Herb Pennock was asked who were the toughest hitters he had faced, he said emphatically, "I just couldn't get Chapman out in the old days. He was so good that he made me pitch badly to him. He was a great player—a really great one. He was like chain lightning going down to first."

In 1932 the issue of beanballs again became a popular pro and con subject with baseball writers across America. In his syndicated column, Wes Pegler, who in the years ahead gained notoriety as an outspoken voice against government and its policies, was clearly against the pitchers who threw at hitters. Pegler wrote, "The death of Chapman was a great shock to the baseball community and although Carl Mays of the Yankees, the pitcher who struck him down and out, insisted that he did not throw to hit him, the suspicion was not so much disproved as it was not proved." Pegler had no doubt in his mind what happened that day.

In an incredible irony, about five years later, Tris Speaker, while doing maintenance at home on his second-floor porch, lost his balance and crashed to the ground, fracturing his skull. He survived the fall, but while he was recuperating his memories of Ray came flooding back. To reporters, he vividly recounted the scene at the New York hospital, claiming to have been at Ray's bedside witnessing his best friend's final moment.

Ray's name made national news in 1937, when Tigers player-manager Mickey Cochrane took a fastball from the Yankees' Bump Hadley in the right temple, suffering a fractured skull and concussion. Most of the initial reports compared the incident to Ray's 1920 fatal beaning, though Hadley was immediately vindicated of any wrongdoing. Seventeen years later, medical procedures were more advanced, allowing doctors to effectively treat the critically injured ballplayer. Cochrane survived the damage but faced a lengthy, difficult recovery.

While still in the baseball business, Steve O'Neill would make a point on his western travels of stopping by Herrin, Illinois, to visit Ray's father and his brother Roy. They would talk about Ray, remembering stories and recounting the great plays he made in the field and at bat. Friends like Jack Graney, Speaker, and O'Neill never forgot their old teammate, still mentioning him in interviews when they were senior citizens.

Mrs. Kathleen Daly lived in the family home until her death in 1950 at eighty-three. The proud old home with all its haunting memories was sold the following year, then razed in the late 1960s. By that time all the upper-class people had moved eastward, to University Heights, Shaker Heights, and even further to millionaire estates in Pepper Pike and Hunting Valley. The Daly house, until its demolition, stood as a reminder of a bygone era, when the rich and powerful ruled the streets of Cleveland.

In August of 1977, almost exactly fifty-seven years from the day of Ray's death, a peculiar story appeared in newspapers around the country. A veteran reporter in Orlando, Florida, claimed that in 1950 he had interviewed Charlie Jamieson, the starting left fielder on the 1920 team, and that Jamieson had possession of the infamous ball that ended Ray's life. While Ray was being carried to the locker room, said the story, the players were milling around home plate, waiting for the game to be resumed, when Jamieson spotted the ball sitting near the batter's box. He picked it up and put it into his back pocket for the rest of the ballgame. He allegedly told the reporter, "After the game I threw the ball into my bag. It remained there for some time. After the World Series, I cleaned out my locker and brought the ball home." At the end of the interview he handed the ball to the reporter to take with him.

From there the story becomes even more bizarre. The writer drove to a high school baseball practice, where he coached the team. One of the players grabbed the ball and used it to hit grounders to the infielders. A bouncer to the third baseman took a weird hop, smacking the player in the eye. Though the ball was hit fairly softly, the young man suffered a fractured cheekbone. The coach-reporter, fearing the ball was jinxed, put it in a cabinet, where it remained untouched ever since.

There was no confirmation of the story, but newspapers around the United States picked it up anyway. Whether Jamieson actually took the ball will likely never be known, as anyone connected to August 16, 1920, has long since passed away. But the idea that the fatal ball is still lingering somewhere is food for thought, at least for the likes of conspiracy theorists and UFO devotees.

In 2006 Ray was elected to the Cleveland Indians Hall of Fame, the first elections held since 1972. The bronze plaque of Ray, dedicated shortly after his death and emblazoned with the words "He lives in the hearts of all who knew him," hangs proudly at Progressive Field for all to see. For years the impressive panel had been lost in storage after being transferred from Municipal Stadium to the then–Jacobs Field. By chance, in 2007 a staff member was rummaging through some neglected, grimy boxes when the plaque miraculously reappeared. After careful restoration it became a permanent fixture in the outdoor Indians/Guardians Hall of Fame.

Back home in Herrin, a portrait sits in a glass case at the high school among all the other sports heroes. Ray still appears in all types of baseball card reprint sets dedicated to players from long ago. On the internet there are numerous images of him in portraits and fielding poses. In many there is an unmistakable smile on his face, one that seems to show how much he relished being a ballplayer.

In 2022 a documentary, *War on the Diamond*, was released illustrating the long rivalry between Cleveland and the New York Yankees. The story begins with the circumstances surrounding Ray's death then proceeds through the years with colorful stories of enmity between the two ball clubs.

When *Baseball Magazine* published their 1920 story on Ray's death, F. C. Lane commented on the photo used to accompany the feature. "From the half dozen pictures of Chapman in our files, we sought one suited to the conventional border of black. But every one of them showed the great Cleveland shortstop with a smile. So, we said why not! In Chapman, the smile was characteristic of the man. So let his friends remember him as he looked in life." Now, 104 years later, the words are still appropriate for the man who left us well before his time.

Sources

BOOKS

Allen, Lee. *The American League Story.* New York: Hill and Wang, 1962.

Benjamin, Ludy T. *A History of Psychology.* New York: McGraw-Hill, 1996.

Bristow, Nancy. *American Pandemic.* New York: Oxford University Press, 2012.

Bundy, Chris. *French Lick Springs Resort.* French Lick: privately printed, 2006.

Lewis, Franklin. *The Cleveland Indians.* New York: Putnam, 1949.

Lieb, Fred. *Baseball As I Have Known It.* New York: Coward, McCann and Geoghegan, 1977.

Ritter, Lawrence. *The Glory of Their Times.* New York: Macmillan, 1966.

Sowell, Mike. *The Pitch That Killed.* Chicago: Ivan R. Dee, 1989.

Stine, Lawrence. *Historic Old West End Toledo, Ohio.* Toledo: Book Masters, 2005.

PERIODICALS

Baseball Magazine (October 1920)
Carbondale Daily Free Press (2018)
Cleveland Leader (1912–17)
Cleveland News (1912–21, 1926, 1928)
Cleveland Plain Dealer (1912–21, 1926, 1928)
Cleveland Press (1912–21, 1926, 1928)
Columbus Dispatch (1912)
Davenport Daily Times (1908–11)
Herrin News (1907, 1915)
Owensboro Messenger (1911–20, 1952)
Sporting News (1912–20)
Toledo Blade (1920)
Toledo News Bee (1911–12)
Toledo Times (1916)

LIBRARIES AND ARCHIVES

Cleveland Public Library
Cleveland Guardians
Cuyahoga County Archives
Cuyahoga County Library
Cuyahoga County Probate Court
Davenport, Iowa, Public Library
Daviess County Public Library
Ellicottville, New York, Historical Society
Herrin City Library
Herrin High School Library
Los Angeles County Archives, California
National Baseball Hall of Fame Library, Cooperstown, New York
     (Player Files)
Old West End Association
Rockefeller Archives Center
Society for American Baseball Research
Toledo Lucas County Public Library
University of Notre Dame Libraries

PERSONAL COMMUNICATIONS

Chapman family
Daly-McMahon families
Margaret Chapman interview courtesy of Bob Becker Video
     Productions

WEBSITES

http://www.baseball-almanac.com

Index

St. Lawrence Hospital (New York, NY), 135, 138
St. Louis, Missouri, 7
St. Louis Browns, 23–24, 28, 32, 80–81, 100–101, 112–13, 127, 132, 144
Stoelzle Hardware baseball team, 5
St. Philomena Church (Cleveland, OH), 56, 121, 146–47, 150, 159
Swayne Field, 16, 18

"Taps" (bugle call), 152
Tenney, Ross, 144
Tesreau, Jeff, 42
Texas, 1, 49, 96–97
Thatcher, Frank, 143
Thomas, Chet, 92
Thomas, Ira, 42, 44
Three-I League, 6–9, 14
thrift stamps, 157
Tobin, Jack, 81
Toledo, OH, 18–19, 56, 76, 86, 90
Toledo Mud Hens, 13–19, 25, 44, 50, 98
Toledo News Bee, 17, 76
Torkelson, Red, 97–98
Turner, Terry, 20–21, 23, 31–32, 37, 82, 84, 101, 105

U-boats, 87, 104
Union Station (Cleveland, OH), 142, 148
United States, 41, 54, 88, 90, 99, 110, 122, 169
United States Army, 94, 99, 104, 106
United States Marines, 125
United States Navy, 103–5, 107

University of Alabama, 125
University of Pittsburgh, 105–6

Veach, Bobby, 5–6, 23, 53
Vitt, Oscar, 33
Volstead Act. *See* Prohibition

Waco, TX, 49
Waddell, Rube, 17, 98
Wade, Jeptha, 147
Wagner, Honus, 26, 36, 51
Walker, Johnny, 160
Walker, Tilly, 131
Walla Walla, WA, 42
Wamby, Bill, 40, 80, 82–83, 85, 93, 97, 101, 103, 106, 108, 113, 126, 133, 154–55, 160
Ward, Aaron, 133
War Department, 102
Warner, Glen, 106
War on the Diamond (film), 170
Washington, D.C., 88, 111
Washington Senators, 24, 32, 40, 42, 50, 56–58, 79, 82–83, 85, 92–93, 96–97, 112, 115, 130–31, 152
Weaver, Buck, 22
Wood, Joe, 31, 88, 108, 112, 115–16, 124, 126–27, 140, 145, 149, 154
workman's compensation, 155
World Series, 42, 108, 115–17, 124, 129
World War I, 2, 87, 111, 135, 157

Young, Ralph, 127

Zachary, Tom, 131